Frederick Porter Smith

A Vocabulary of Proper Names, in Chinese and English, of Places, Persons, Tribes, and Sects

In China, Japan, Corea, Annam, Siam, Burmah, the Straits and Adjacent

Countries

Frederick Porter Smith

A Vocabulary of Proper Names, in Chinese and English, of Places, Persons, Tribes, and Sects
In China, Japan, Corea, Annam, Siam, Burmah, the Straits and Adjacent Countries

ISBN/EAN: 9783337167998

Printed in Europe, USA, Canada, Australia, Japan

Cover: Foto ©Thomas Meinert / pixelio.de

More available books at **www.hansebooks.com**

A VOCABULARY OF PROPER NAMES,

IN CHINESE AND ENGLISH,

OF

PLACES, PERSONS, TRIBES, AND SECTS,

IN CHINA, JAPAN, COREA, ANNAM, SIAM, BURMAH,

THE STRAITS AND ADJACENT COUNTRIES.

COMPILED BY

F. PORTER SMITH, M. B. Lond.

Medical Missionary in China.

———•••———

SHANGHAI:
PRESBYTERIAN MISSION PRESS.
1870.

THIS VOCABULARY IS RESPECTFULLY INSCRIBED,

BY PERMISSION,

TO

S. WELLS WILLIAMS, Esq., L. L. D.

&c., &c.,

Secretary of the Legation of the United States, Peking,

by his obliged friend

THE COMPILER.

PREFACE.

THIS Chinese and English list of proper names of places, persons, dynasties, tribes and sects, having interest or relation to both Chinese and foreigners, was begun to be compiled in ignorance of the existence of a somewhat similar appendix to a work on Chinese topography, by the learned and indefatigable author of the "Middle Kingdom." It professes to treat briefly of those unusual designations, called 別名 *pieh ming*, of places in China Proper, which often puzzle readers and translators, and of the names of those colonial or semi-dependent states which now do, or formerly did, range themselves around the "favoured nation" more directly ruled by the Emperor of China. Names of places, etc., in Corea, Burmah, Siam, Malaysia, India, and Asia in general, have been added, together with stray names of western countries and peoples who have, or had, relations with China. In this way it is hoped that the list may be advantageously consulted as a supplement to the dictionaries of the Chinese language, not hitherto supplied with this convenient arrangement. Matters of historical, classical, geographical, and commercial interest, and some of the important changes wrought in Turkestan and Central Asia by the joint action of Mohammedan disaffection and Russian enterprise, have been occasionally introduced, so as to bring the information up to the most recent dates. Japanese names, as written in Chinese, have been conveniently incorporated, and the most important places in China mentioned in Marco Polo's writings have been emphasised. Traces of the profession of the compiler will be occasionally met with in the shape of short references to drugs. To the labours of

Duhalde, Morrison, Davis, Williams, Legge, Julien, Pauthier, Wylie, Edkins, Mayers, Williamson, and a score of contributors to the literature of the subjects involved, the compiler is almost entirely indebted for what is valuable in this brief summary. At the same time it is but fair to state that, as often as possible, the original Chinese and other works treating upon the matters in hand, have been carefully examined. To the contributors to the "Chinese Repository," Dennys's "Treaty Ports of China and Japan," the "Notes and Queries on China and Japan," and the "Transactions of the North China Branch of the Royal Asiatic Society," as well as to the exhaustive works of Max Müller, much obligation is freely confessed. An index has been provided as a means of reference for those who are more familiar with the names of places used in foreign works, than with the ordinary phonetic equivalent of the Chinese character. Some Chinese names included in the text will also be found in the index, which should be consulted in cases where the alphabetical series has failed to afford the clue. For almost all other occasions it is hoped that the list, arranged alphabetically according to the mandarin pronunciation, may be found convenient and instructive to those who, like the compiler, are engaged in their earlier studies of a Babel tongue.

Hankow, March 31st, 1870.

F. P. S.

A LIST OF CHINESE PROPER NAMES

ENGLISH EQUIVALENTS.

———•••———

A

呵 此 釐 國 A-ch'ih-li kwoh, a country on the Coromandel coast of South India, said to yield the best olibanum. There is an *A-ki-ni*, which has been identified with Kharashar.

阿 城 A-ching, or O-fang-kung, the palace or harem of Ts'in-chi-hwang at Si-ngan fu, in Shensi.

阿 克 蘇 城 A-keh-suh ching, Aksu, or Oksu in Chinese Tartary, the Auxasia of Ptolemy, an important town, containing 20,000 people, more civilized than those of the remaining districts of *Sin Kiang*. It lies on the great road to Ili, in Lat. 41° 09′ N., and Long. 19° 13′ E., to the east of Ushi. The district of the same name is bounded E. by the petty chiefdoms of Bai and Sairim: S. by the desert, and on the west by Ushi.

阿 克 但 河 A-keh-tan ho, or the Alotan river, one of the sources of the Yellow River.

阿 關 A-kwan, or O-kwan, a name of Shensi province, or thereabouts, during the Ts'in dynasty.

阿 拉 善 額 魯 特 旗 A-la-shen ngeh-lu-teh k'i, or the banner of the Alashan Eleuths. Their country lies west of Ninghia fu in Kansuh, and north of the Great Wall, as far as Gobi.

阿 革 楚 克 城 A-leh-tsu-keh ching or Altchucu, one of the seven garrisons in Kirin, lying at the mouth of the river of the same name, a branch of the Songari, E.N.E. of Petuné.

阿 里 城 A-li ching, Ari, or Nari, a district and town of Ulterior Thibet, is an extensive but thinly-settled region, containing tracts of desert land, stretching from Tsang to Ladak. It borders on Badakshan and Cashmere on the west.

阿 魯 A-lu, a kingdom of Sumatra, to the E. of Acheen.

阿 魯 科 爾 沁 A-lu-ko-rh-tsin, or Aru Korchin, the north Korchins, a tribe of Mongols in Inner Mongolia.

亞 媽 澳 A-ma-ngau, the port of the goddess A-ma, the name which is probably the origin of the name of the island and port of Macao.

阿彌陀佛 A-mi-to-fuh, or Ta-mi-to, Amita-bha, or Amita Buddha of the west.

安端 An-tan, or Ngan-tan, the Roman emperor Marcus Aurelius Antoninus, who sent an embassy to China, A.D. 161-6. This name is sometimes written *An-tun*.

阿霸哈納爾 A-pa-ha-nah-rh, or Abaganar, a tribe of the fourth corps of Inner Mongolia, divided into two banners, and lying north of Tsakhar, and 640 *li* N. E. of Kalgan.

阿霸垓 A-pa-kai, the Abagais, a tribe of the fourth corps of Inner Mongolia, living between Tsakhar, or Chahar, and Gobi, 590 *li* N.E. of Kalgan.

阿霸科爾 A-pa-ko-rh, the country of Bokhara, called also *Pou-ho-rh*.

阿爾但河 A-rh-tan ho, a name of the Yellow River in its early course. See A-kch-tan ho.

阿丹 A-tan, or O-tan, the Mahommedan name for Adam in Chinese. This is also the name of a country, mentioned in the Pen T'sao as furnishing the medicine, called 羚羊角, Ling-yang-koh, or antelope-horn. See O-tan.

阿瓦 A-wa, Ava, or Aungwa, the capital city and kingdom of Burmah, formerly including Pegu and Arracan. See Mien-tien, or Mien kwoh.

阿邑 A-yih, or O-yih, the name of Tung-o hien, or Yang-kuh hien, in Shantung province, during the Confucian period. See Tung-o hien.

C

乍浦 Cha-pu, the port of Hang-chau, or *Cha-pu chin*, "the mart of Cha-pu," whence trade is carried on with Japan. This is not to be confounded with the *Canfu* of Marco Polo. See Kan-pu.

乍丫 Cha-ya, or Jaya, a town and district in Thibet, inhabited by mountaineers, partially independent of Chinese rule.

察哈爾 Chah-ha-rh, Chahar or Tsakhar, a district lying north of Shansi, inhabited by the Tsakhar tribe of Mongols, whose pastures are included in Chihli province. They make up eight banners, and are controlled by an officer at *Chang-kia* gate.

閘河 Chah-ho, the "River of Locks," the Grand Canal, upon which there were at least ten large locks under as many officers. See Yun-liang ho.

扎賴特 Chah-lai-teh, the Tchalits, a Mongolian tribe, on the west of the Nonni river, west of Kirin ula.

扎魯特 Chah-lu-teh, the Djarots, a Mongol tribe dwelling 1,100 *li* N.E. of Hi-fung gate, in the Great Wall, and west of Shingking.

察木多城 Chah-muh-to ching, Tsiando, or Chamdo, a military post, the capital of Kham, in the N.W. of Anterior Thibet.

扎什城 Chah-shih ching, Chashi, or Djassi, a district and town of Anterior Thibet, N.W. of H'lassa, and the seat of a small Chinese garrison.

扎什倫佈城 Chah-shih lun-pu ching, Teshu h'lumba, or Zhikatsé-jung, the capital city of Tsang, or Ulterior Thibet, 26 miles west of H'lassa, and the residence of the *teshu-*

lama, or *banchin erdeni*. It contains some three or four hundred houses, with palaces, convents, and mausolea, and is situated in the fertile basin of the Yaru-tsangbu, in Lat. 29° 4′ 90″ N., and Long. 80° 7′ E. A large trade was carried on hence to the mouth of the Ganges. The teshu-lama is in *some* sense more important than his more political colleague, the *dalai-lama*.

扎 錫 岡 Chah-sih-kang, Teshigang, a district in Thibet.

長 春 廳 Chang-chun ting, in Kirin, one of the smallest of the three *ting* departments of that province, lying on its western borders, due west of Kirin ula, and on the west of the Songari river.

長 崎 Chang-k'i, the port of Nagasaki in Japan.

彰 郡 Chang-kiun, one of Ts'in Chi-hwang's prefectures, answering to a part of Yang-chau of Yü's time.

張 家 口 Chang-kia-k'au, a pass in the Great Wall, near which is Kalgan, a large town on the line of the caravan road prescribed in the new Russo-Chinese treaty, in the department of *Kau-peh-tan*, in Chihli. Lat. 40° 54′ N., and Long. 114° 50′ E. *Kalga* is the Mongol word for a mart. Native soda is largely exported from this town.

長 江 Chang-kiang, the "Long River," the Yangtsz'. See Ta Kiang.

昌 國 Chang kwoh, the sub-prefecture of *Ting-hai ting* in Chekiang.

長 安 Chang-ngan, the name of the old capital of Shensi province, also the capital of China, in the T'sin, Han, Sui, and T'ang periods. It was known to the Nestorians as *Khoubdam*, or *Koumdam*. The province is still called by this name in official documents, and it is continued as the name of a district.

長 白 山 Chang-peh shan, the southern extremity of the range of *Sih-hih-tih* mountains, near the Corean frontier. The perennial snows of this mountain have rendered it a mark of veneration. It was the home of the Manchu race.

昌 圖 廳 Chang-t'u ting, a district of Fung-t'ien fu, in Shingking.

長 夜 Chang-ye, a mart on the "Western Borders," for traffic between the 44 tribes of *Fan* and *Hwaitsz'*, and the Chinese.

兆 府 Chau fu, see Kiang-chau fu.

州 湄 Chau-mei, a place to the N. of *Puh-ni* on Chinese maps, and probably identical with *Chiang-mai*, the capital of North Laos.

舟 山 Chau shan, or "Boat Island," the largest island of the Chusan Archipelago. The district-town of Tinghai, lying on the southern side of the island, is the capital.

朝 鮮 Chau-sien, the Chinese official name of Corea, as a tribute-bearing country. It is divided into eight provinces, called *tau*. See Kau-li kwoh.

朝 鮮 天 毒 Chau-sien-t'ien-tuh, a name of India. See T'ien tuh.

爪 哇 Chau-wa, the island of Java, sometimes called Ye-po-thi, or Yava-dwipa. See Koh-lah-pa.

昭 烏 達 盟 Chau-wu-tah ming, one of the six *ming*, or corps of Inner Mongolia, living towards the N.E. of that country.

爪 亞 Chau-ya, the Javanese. See Chau-wa.

車 師 國 Chè-sz' kwoh, the capital and country of the *Tuh-kiueh*, or Turkic tribes of Central

Asia, during the fifth century. See Wu-lu-moh-tsi.

占城 Chen ching, a place described as peopled by the Laos tribes, and answering to some such town as Saigon. It is however commonly referred to Tsiampa, formerly an independent portion of Cochin China. See Shi-pí. Cambodia is sometimes called Chen-lah, instead of Chin-lah. Lin-yih may have been in Tsiampa.

占卑 Chen-pi, Tsiampa. See Chen ching, and Ping-shun chin.

瞻德城 Chen-teh ching, a garrison town in Ili, situated N.W. of Hwuiyuen ching, to which it is attached.

芝罘 Chi-fau, or Chefoo, a harbour in the same bay as Yentai, the actual port, misnamed Chefoo. There is a point near this, called Chefoo Cape.

哲里木盟 Chi-li-muh ming, one of the six corps of Inner Mongolia, living on the borders of Kirin and Shingking.

支那 Chi-na, an Indian name for China. See Chin-tan.

知汶 Chi-wan, the island of Timor, one of the principal sources of sandal-wood.

赤縣神州 Chih-hien-shin-chau, an old name of China.

赤泥 Ch'ih-ni, a Mohammedan name of China. See Tung-t'u.

拓跋 Ch'ih-pah, a race descended from the Tung-lu, or, as some say, the descendants of old Hwang-ti.

直省 Ch'ih sang, a collective name of all the provinces of China Proper. See Shih-pah-sang.

赤土 Ch'ih-t'u, a country in the "Southern Sea," near Fu-nan, and probably identical with Sien-lo, or Siam. See Sien-lo.

陳 Chin, the capital of Fuh-hi, near K'ai-fung fu (Honan).

眞州 Chin-chau, the district of I'-ching, in Yang-chau fu. See Lwan-kiang and Yang-tsz' kiang.

鎮江 Chin-kiang, a treaty-port and prefectural city, near the joining of the Grand Canal and the Yang-tsz' kiang.

眞臘 Chin-lah, or 占臘 Chen-lah, the kingdom of Cambodia, lying between Annam and Siam. It was first tributary to, and then absorbed by the state of Fu-nan. See Tung-p'u-chai.

鎮西 Chin-si, the department of Chin-si fu, in Kansuh, sometimes called Barkul.

震旦 Chin-tan, an Indian name for China. See Chi-na.

鄭芝龍 Ching Chi-lung, the name of the father of Koxinga, the Formosan chief, whose own name was Ching Ching-lung, and that of his son, Ching K'i-shwang, who received the title of Wang, on his submission.

成吉思汗 Ching-kih-sz'-han, Genghis Khan, the Greatest (or Strongest) Khan, the style of Temugin, grandsire of Kublai Khan. See Teh-mah-chin.

承德縣 Ching-teh hien, in Shingking, belonging to Fung-t'ien fu, in Lat. 41° 06′ N., and Long. 117° 46′ E.

成都府 Ching-tu fu, or Yih chau in Sechuen. See next.

成都路 Ching-tu lu, the province of Sechuen under the Mongols, called Sardansu by Marco Polo. Ching-tu is still the name of the capital of Sechuen. It is the Sin-du-fu of Marco

Polo, was the capital of the After Han dynasty, and is still a fine city.

綽 羅 斯 部 Choh-lo-sz' pu, the Choros tribes, arranged under two standards, living in the south of Kokonor. The word *pu* stands for aimak, i. e. tribes of Persia.

卓 索 圖 盟 Choh-soh-t'u ming, the Choshots, one of the six corps of Inner Mongolia, living in the S.W. of that country.

諸 番 Chü Fan, a collective name for all foreign countries. See Nui fan.

諸 夏 Chü Hia, "All the Chinas," a name of the Chinese Empire.

樞 密 副 使 博 羅 Chü-mih fuh-sz' poh-lo, the style and name of Marco Polo, the Venetian traveller, as "junior envoy" "and privy councillor," accredited to the King of Annam, from Kublai Khan. See Poh-lo.

朱 仙 鎮 Chü-sien chin, one of the four marts in China, to the S. of K'ai-fung fu, (Honan).

朱 波 地 Chu-po-ti, an old name of the kingdom of Burmah.

出 島 Chuh-t'au, the artificial fan shaped island of Desima, near the city of Nagasaki, the prison of the Portuguese and Dutch traders in Japan. See P'ing-hu-t'au.

準 喝 爾 Chun-kieh-rh, Soungar, the name of an extinct tribe of I'li. See T'ien-shan-peh-lu.

中 州 Chung chau, an old name for Honan province, still used in documents. This is the foundation and seat of that "central region" which grew into the *Chung kwoh*, which see.

中 興 府 Chung-hing fu, the capital of the Hia kingdom, the Calatia of Marco Polo, and now called *Ninghia*, the head of a department in Kansuh. It was also formerly called *Hwai-yuen*.

中 華 Chung hwa, "Central Flower," a name of Honan province, extended to China at large. China is called *Nikan Kurun* in Manchu. See Chung-yuen.

重 慶 Ch'ung-king, a prefectural city in Sechuen, 720 miles from Hankow, and 6,670 *li* from Peking. It stands at the point of junction of the Kia-ling river with the Yang-tsz', and receives the traffic of one third of the province.

中 國 Chung kwoh, China, the "Middle Kingdom." See Chung-yuen and Chung chau. This name would appear to be applied to India by Fah-hien, in his Fuh-kwoh-ki.

中 山 Chung shan, the "Central Mount," on which is built the capital of the kingdom of Lew-chew. See Shau-ni and Liu-kiu kwoh.

中 天 竺 Chung-t'ien chuh, Central India, answering to the once powerful state of Malwah. See T'ien chuh kwoh, and Si T'ien.

中 都 Chung-tu, a town in the old state of Lu, of which Confucius was made governor. See Ping-luh.

中 原 Chung-yuen, an old name of Honan province, afterwards applied to the whole of China. For many years before the final subjugation of the numerous nations of the "Eastern foreigners," by the Han emperors, China was in another sense a "middle kingdom," between these and the Miautsz' and other tribes.

F

梵 Fan, the country of Magadha. It also stands for the Pali and for the Sanscrit languages. Fan is said to be an abbreviation of *Fan-lan-mo*, or Brahma.

樊城 Fan ching. See Siang-ho.

梵僧 Fan-sang, the Bonzes, or Buddhist priests in China and Japan. These Chinese words are pronounced *Bonsu* in Japan, and were thence probably introduced by the Portuguese into China.

番都城 Fan-t'u ching, the capital city of Bokhara.

藩陽 Fan-yang, a name of Fung-t'ien fu or Shingking pun ching. It was one of the ca pitals of the Wei princes.

范陽 Fan-yang, the chief department and capital of the prefecture of Yu chau under T'sin Chi-hwang, answering to what is now Shun-I'hien and Ting-hing hien in Chihli.

番禺 Fan-yu, the capital of Kiau chau, one of the provinces of the Tsin dynasty.

浮屠 Fau-t'u, a name of Buddha, sometimes given to Buddhist priests.

費雅喀 Fei-ya-k'eh, a hunting tribe on the Sagalien river.

扶魯爾 Fu-lu-rh, a Mahomraedan tribe, to the W. of Yarkand.

扶南 Fu-nan, an old Cambodian kingdom to which Chin-lah was annexed. It lay some 7,000 *li* to the S.W. of Jeh-nan, and more than 3,000 *li* to the S.W. of Lin-yih. See Kih kwoh.

扶桑國 Fu-sang kwoh, or 佛桑國 Fuh-sang kwoh, a country named after the Fu-sang shrub, a Malvaceous genus (Althœa rosea?), and producing reddish pears, excellent grapes, cream, or kumiss, and abounding in valuable metals, but without iron. It is said to be 25,000 *li* to the E. of China. A Buddhist priest, named Hwui-shin, came to China from thence, during the T'si dynasty.

富士山 Fu-sz' shan, the Fusiyama (mountain) in Japan.

扶餘 Fu-yu, or 夫餘 a country to the N. of Kau-ku-li, related to Peh-tsí. It is said to have belonged to Yuen-t'u.

福 Fuh. This word when found on Chinese cash, stands for Fuhkien, one of the 25 Chinese mints in Kanghi's time.

福州 Fuh-chau, or Hok-chiu hu, the "Happy region," the capital of Fukien, in Lat. 26° 5′ N., and Long. 119° 20′ E. Yung ching and San shan are names of this departmental city.

復州 Fuh-chau, a sub-department of Fung-t'ien fu in Shingking.

復州城 Fuh chau ching, a garrison in Shingking, subordinate to the Shingking-pun-ching.

佛教 Fuh kiau, the Buddhist religion. See San kiau and Shih kiau.

佛國 Fuh-kwoh, the "Buddhist country" of India.

佛狼機 Fuh-lang-ki, the Feringhis or Franks, a name given to the Portuguese in 1517, on their landing in China, under Fernao Peres de Andrado. This was the first formal intercourse of modern European nations with the Chinese of the south, ending in a permanent establishment. Raphael Perestrello, a descendant of Columbus, had previously reached in 1516, one of the islands at the mouth of the Canton River. See Sih-tsz'-nien.

佛狼西 Fuh-lang-si, a name given to the French and their country, and to other western nations. See Ta fah kwoh.

福老 Fuh-lau, or Hoklo, the people of *Ch'au-chow*, in the N.E. of Canton province. They prevail in the *Luhfung, Haifung* and *Kweishan* districts of *Hweichau fu*. They are said to have come from Fukien, some five or six centuries ago. They speak the Tiechiu dialect, which is quite distinct from that of the Hakkas or Puntis. They are a bold, cruel and marauding race. See Keh-kia.

栱林國 Fuh-lin-kwoh, or Pih-lin-kwoh, a country said to be related to Persia, but of a different language. It has been variously identified with Palestine, Syria and the Roman empire. Pauthier suggests that the words point to Constantinople, as the capital (polin), of the Byzantine empire. It seems more likely that the name refers to the Philistines (Phu-listiemi), who gave their name to Palestine. They were of Hamitic origin, and their name occurs as Phut, in connexion with Persia in Ezekiel xxvii. 10. They had large navies, and rich fleets of merchantmen in many seas. They are very likely to have been confused or conjoined with their northern neighbours the Phœnicians, whose name sufficiently resembles the Chinese Fuh-lin. Herodotus says that the Phœnicians had migrated from the Red Sea at an early period. The Persian gulf as one arm of the Red Sea, would bring them into connexion with Persia. Phœnician numerals resemble the Chinese forms somewhat.

佛泥 Fuh-ni, a country to the S.E. of Canton, answering to Borneo. See Puh-ni.

佛山 Fuh-shan, or Fatshan, near Canton, one of the largest marts of the empire. The expression 五鎮 Wu chin, or "five guards," or five protecting hills is applied to five celebrated subordinate peaks.

鳳凰廳 Fung-hwang ting, in Shingking, department of Fung-t'ien fu, lies on the eastern frontier, near the Yahlung river, and monopolizes all the trade with Corea.

奉天府 Fung-t'ien fu, in Shingking, is the Chinese name for Moukden, the capital of Manchuria. It lies in Lat. 41° 50′ 30″ N., and Long. 123° 37′ 30″ E. It is the capital of a very large department. It was also called Fan-yang in the Wei and Mongolian periods.

H

哈喇沙拉 Ha-la-sha-la. See Kharashar.

哈密 Ha-mih, or Hamil, a town included in Kansuh, W. of the Great Wall, belonging to the district of Barkul, or Chin-si. It formerly belonged to the Songares, an Eleuthian tribe, now scattered. It is pleasantly situated in Lat. 42°, 1,600 *li* beyond the gate called Kia-yu-kwan. See I-wu-lu.

哈薩克 Ha-sah-keh, the Hassacks, or Cossacks, sometimes called Sara Kaizak, or "robbers of the desert." They lived, originally, between the Ob and Yenesei rivers, where Mongolic tribes settled among them. They now occupy part of Bokhara and Kokand, N.W. of Tarbagatai in Songaria.

海城縣 Hai-ching hien, in Shingking, department of Fung-t'ien fu.

海口 Hai-k'au, or Hoihau, a seaport in the island of Hainan.

海岸 Hai-ngan, the coast-line of the "Eastern Sea," drawn on Chinese maps.

海西國 Hai-si kwoh, a name of Ta-ts'in, lying W. of the Caspian Sea, the limit of Chinese adventure, according to some. The name sounds like Asia. See Li-han.

海島 Hai-t'au, a name usually referred to the islands on the E. of China. This term is translated by Staunton in his "Tartar Code" as "foreign islands." See Tau-i.

海塘 Hai-t'ang, the "Sea-bund" formed in the 7th century along the bay of Hang-chow, to resist the action of the high tides.

海牙國 Hai-ya kwoh, Herat, or Heri, the ancient Aria, the Haroyu of the Zend Avesta, from whence assafœtida used to come to China.

漢川 Han-ch'uen, a name of Han-chung fu in Shensi. There is a district of this name in Hupeh.

漢中 Han-chung in Shensi, the Cancun of Marco Polo. This was the name of one of Ts'in Chi-hwang's 40 prefectures, forming a part of Yung chau, or Ho-si. See Hing-yuen lu.

瀚海 Han hai, the narrow westerly portion of the great Desert of Gobi. See Ko-pih. The Chan-t'ang or Aksai-chin, commencing near Rodok, is said by some to join Gobi. See Lo-to-keh ching.

漢口 Han-k'au, or 漢皋 Han-kau, the port of Hankow, at the mouth of the Han river, distant from Shanghai 582 geographical miles, and situated in Lat. 30° 32′ 51″ N., and Long. 114° 19′ 55″ E. As one of the largest marts in China it is called 漢鎮 Han-chin. As the Han, from its mouth to the large city of Siang-yang fu, is sometimes spoken of as the Siang ho, so Hankow is often called in old writings Siang-ho-k'au, or Siang-k'au. It is also spoken of as 九省通衢, Kiu-sang-t'ung-k'u, or 五方雜處, Wu-fang-tsah-ch'u, terms signifying that it is the great thoroughfare of half of China, and the residence of a mixture of folks from all quarters. Hankow was anciently called Hia-k'au and Mien-k'au.

函谷關 Han-kuh kwan. See Kwan.

漢南 Han-nan, a name of King chau, under the Shang dynasty.

漢津 Han-tsin, the name by which the Han-yang hien was known before the T'ang dynasty. See Ts'ing-ch'uen.

漢土 Han-t'u, the Japanese name for China.

度都斯但 Han-t'u-sz'-tan, Hindostan. See Wan-t'u-sz' tan.

漢陽關 Han-yang kwan, the name of an ancient barrier in Pau-ching hien (Shensi), which probably gave its name to the prefecture of Han-yang, formerly spoken of as a part of Kiang-hia kiun. This latter name is now confined to a district in Wuchang fu. See Han-kau, T'sing-ch'uen, Tun-yang and Han-tsin.

恒河 Hang-ho, the sacred river of India, the Ganges. The Chinese name is nearly the same as "Gunga," the Go-go, meaning the "Ceaseless River." A Chinese number called 恒 河 沙, extends to fifty-three places of figures.

鎬 京 Hau-king, the capital of Wu-wang, identified with Si King, or Chang-ngan (Shensi).

後 藏 Hau-tsang. See Si-tsang.

黑 龍 江 Heh-lung kiang, the Amur, Yamur, or Sagalien Ula ("Black River.") The Chinese name signifies "Black Dragon River." It is the sixth in rank of Asian rivers. After joining the Songari river it is called 混 同, Kwan-t'ung. It rises in the Kenteh spur of the Daourian mountains, and has a course of more than 2,000 miles to the sea. Amur is the equivalent of Ta Kiang, or "Great River," a name well deserved from the large area it drains, as well as from the extent of its tributaries.

黑 龍 江 城 Heh-lung-kiang ching, the chief town of the N.E. division of Tsitsihar, which lies on the Amur, in Lat. 50° N., and Long. 127° E. It is sometimes called Sagalien ula, and is used as a penal settlement for Chinese criminals.

黑 水 Heh shwui, a name of the Kin-sha-kiang. The Moh-hoh were called Heh-shwui Moh-hoh during the Sui dynasty, from a place in Shingking.

奚 霫 Hi-chih, an ancient tribe of the T'ang period, on the N.E., near Corea.

熙 春 城 Hi-ch'un ching, a garrison and penal settlement, lying due N. of Hwuiyuen.

喜 峯 口 Hi-fung k'au, the most easterly pass in the Great Wall, in Lat. 40° 26′ N.

奚 國 Hi kwoh, the country of Siberia.

希 利 尼 Hi-li-ni, the ordinary transference into Chinese of the name of the Hellenes, or Greeks. The ancient Greeks knew nothing of China, and China knew nothing of them perhaps. See Wu-chi-kwoh.

希 百 來 Hi-peh-lai, the usual way of writing the word Hebrew in Chinese translations.

蝦 夷 Hia-i, or "Crab Barbarians," the Chinese name for the natives of Yesso. They are also called Ainos.

厦 門 Hia-men, the port of Amoy, one of the best on the coast; the *Taitun* of Marco Polo. By some Taitun is referred to Chinchew. See T'siuen-chau fu.

厦 島 Hia t'au, the island of Amoy, sometimes called Lu-men or Lu-tau, containing the city of the same name on the S.W. corner. The trade of Amoy once extended to Persia, India, and Malaysia. Marco Polo speaks of two ports under the name of Taitun, or Zaitun.

香 港 Hiang-kiang, or Hong Kong, the island of "Fragrant streams," situated at the mouth of the Canton river, in Lat. 22° 26′ 30″ N., and Long. 114° 08′ 30″ E.

梟 羅 個 沒 里 Hiau-lo-ko-muh-li, the Chinese name of the place from whence the Kara Kitan, or Tungusic progenitors of the Liau dynasty came. It was situated somewhere in the mountains north of Corea, from whence they descended into the provinces in Tartary, called after their dynastic name Liau-tung and Liau-si, and other provinces in northern China. They were called by the Nu-chin, the ancestors of the Kin and Manchu dynasties, Kara Kitai, or Black Tartars, after their subjection in the 11th century. They reigned by nine princes for 200 years, under the name of the Liau dynasty, over an empire in the north of China, which reached also to Kashgar and the T'sung-ling mountains in the west. Their descendants, further scattered by Genghis Khan, are now met with as Mohammedans all over Ili, and in Darbend, near the Caspian Sea. See K'i-tan.

縣 度 Hien-tu, the Hindoo Kush mountains.

咸 陽 Hien-yang, the name of Si-ngan fu (Shensi), as the capital of China under the Ts'in rule, in B.C. 249.

獫 狁 Hien-yun, the Hiung-nu, or Huns of the Chau dynasty, notorious for their savagery and insubordination in the time of Confucius. They are confounded with the Tah-tsu.

與 京 城 Hing-king ching, subordinate to Shingking pun ching in a military point of view, is the family residence of the Manchu emperors of China, and their burial place. It is pleasantly situated in a valley, about sixty miles E. of Moukden.

與 京 理 事 廳 Hing-king-li-sz' ting, one of the three *ting* departments of Shingking, containing the town just mentioned. It is the healthiest part of Manchuria, which enjoys no great reputation for friendliness to man.

與 元 路 Hing-yuen-lu, the province of Cuncun of Marco Polo, in Shensi, now the prefecture of Han-chung.

學 老 Hioh-lau, a name of the Hoklo people. See Fuh-lau.

葷 粥 Hiun-chuh, a *pieh ming* of the Hiung-nu.

休 屠 Hiu-chu, a regal title or style among the Hiung-nu. See Shan-yu, or Tan-yu.

獯 鬻 Hiun-yuh, a name of the Turkic Hiung-nu, under the Hia dynasty.

匈 奴 Hiung-nu, the name of the Turkic tribes, during the Ts'in and Han dynasties. They are identified by Chinese historians with the 山 戎, Shan-jung of the "five emperors," the 葷 粥, Hiun-chuh of Hwang-ti, the 獯 鬻, Hiun-yuh, the 淳 維, Chun-wei (Hia), the 鬼 方, Kwei-fang (Yin), the 獫 狁, Hien-yun (Chau), and the 突 厥, Tuh-kiueh of the Sui and T'ang periods. They founded an empire (B.C. 206) comprising a large portion of Central Asia, on the western borders of China. They were defeated, after frequent warfare with Chinese, in the middle of the 1st century after Christ. Divided into a northern and a southern empire, they were successfully driven from their territories, and forced to migrate westwards. 休 屠, Hiu-chu and 單 于 Shan-yu were regal titles or styles of their empire among them. See Oh-shi.

匈 奴 中 海 Hiung-nu chung hai, the "Sea of Hunland," or Lake of Barkul. It gives its name to the surrounding district, which is more under cultivation near the lake.

熊 岳 城 Hiung-yoh ching in Shingking, a garrison subordinate to Shingking pun ching.

河 Ho, the Ho, or river *par excellence*, the Yellow River. See Hwang ho.

火 州 Ho chau, the "Fire district," a name of the district of Bischbalik, or Turfan ting in Barkul, so called from the volcanic character of the country.

河 中 府 Ho-chung fu, the *Cacian fu* of Marco Polo, the P'u-chau fu of Shansi, of the present time.

和 克 齊 Ho-keh-tsi, Cogacin, the fifth son of Kublai Khan, and viceroy of Yunnan.

何 國 Ho kwoh, a country in the "Western borders," connected with Sogdiana.

荷 蘭 國 Ho-lan kwoh, Holland. See Hung-mau.

火 林 Ho-lin, the ancient Kara korum, the "Black City," the capital of the Mongols, or descendants of Genghis Khan, where only a new khan could be chosen, and invested with the government of an empire which extended from China to Poland, from India to Siberia. It is in Lat. 46° 40′ N., and Long. 102° 50′ E. See Ho-ning.

和寧 Ho-ning, a name given to the city of *Kara korum*, after the defeat of the Mongols. Some uncertainty exists as to its exact situation, which was between the Orkhun and Ta-mir. Kara korum is sometimes called Oranbaligh.

河北 Ho-peh, an ancient province, about A.D. 200, now merged into Shansi. The Ho-peh tau of later date included places in Pehchihli.

和碩恭親王 Ho-shih kung-t‘sin wang, the title of Prince Kung, uncle of the present emperor of China. See Kung-t‘sin-wang.

和碩特部 Ho-shih-teh pu, the tribes of Hoshoits, living on the north and west of the Azure sea. They are arranged with the Tourgouths, Kalkas and other Mongolian tribes under twenty-nine standards, and ruled by the Manchu general residing at Si-ning fu.

火神教 Ho-shin kiau, the religion of the Parsees, worshippers of the "fire spirit."

河西 Ho-si, Tangut, or Tocharia, a region N. of Kokonor, and N.W. of Shensi, the country of the Uigurs. Yü's province of K‘i chau was divided by him into *Ho-tung* and *Ho-si*.

河套 Ho-t‘au, the "River's bend," a name given to the bend of the Yellow River, outside the Great Wall, in the country of the Ortous Mongols, N. of Shensi.

河底江 Ho-ti kiang, a river near Yuen-kiang chau (Yunnan), also called the Sang-koi, and running into the Gulf of Tonquin.

和闐城 Ho-tien ching, Hoten, or Khoten, a large district on the S.W. of the desert of Gobi, embracing all the country S. of Oksu and Yarkand, along the northern base of the Kwanlun mountains, for more than three hundred miles from E. to W. The town of the same name, now called Ilchi, is in an extensive plain on the Khoten river, in Lat. 37° N., and Long. 80° 35′ E. After the Tungani insurrection against Chinese rule in 1862, the Mufti Haji Habeeboolla was made governor of Khoten. He has since been murdered by Yakoob Beg, the conqueror of all Chinese Turkestan. Khoten produces fine linen and cotton stuffs, jade ornaments, copper, grain and fruits. The English word *cotton* may have been derived from the name of this place, which is not far from Kau-chang, the country of the Uigurs who first utilized this staple.

河東 Ho-tung, a part of the present provinces of Shansi and Shantung, anciently forming a *tau*, or province.

河源 Ho-yuen, a part of the "head waters" of the Yellow River. There is a Ho-yuen hien in Canton province.

合州河 Hoh-chau ho, a name of the Kia-ling kiang, which joins the Ta Kiang at Chung-king. It rises in Shensi, and is afterwards joined by the Si-han (Kansuh), Fan-kiang and K‘u-kiang rivers.

霍罕 Hoh-han, or Kokand, the ancient Ferganah, a kingdom under the protection of Russia, lying between Bokhara and Kashgar, and fertilized by the waters of the Jaxartes. Its modern capital lies in a fruitful plain in Lat. 41° 40′ N., and Long. 69° 50′ E. Clover, hemp, and many important plants and trees, having the word *hu* before them, came from here. See Ta-yuen kwoh.

闔 蘇 Hoh-su, Khojend, or Kokand. See Ta-yuen kwoh.

許 Hu, the capital of the Wei state, one of the San kwoh of the latter end of the Tung Han period. It corresponded to the Hu chau or Hu chang, 許昌, near K'ai-fung fu. (Honan).

湖廣 Hu-kwang, the old designation of the two provinces of Hupeh and Hunan.

呼蘭城 Hu-lan ching, the garrison of one of the six commanderies of Tsitsihar, or Heh-lung kiang. The town is small and recently built, and lies S.E. of Tsitsihar, on the Son-gari river, opposite Altchucu. Here the officer resides to control the tribes in the vicinity.

呼倫貝爾城 Hu-lun-pei-rh ching, Hurun-pir, the smallest and most westerly of the six districts of Tsitsihar, lying on a branch of the Amur, W. of the Inner Hing-ngan range. The name is compounded of those of two of its lakes, the Hurun or Kerlon, and the Pir. It is bounded by the Tse tsen Khanate on the W.

滬瀆 Hu-tuh, an old name of Shanghai.

弘法 Hung-fah, or Koübo, the inventor of the Japanese syllabary, called *hirakana*. See Shuh-chau. He lived in China about A.D. 804.

紅海 Hung hai, the Red Sea, answering to the Erythræum Mare of Herodotus, with its two arms, the Persian Gulf, or Eastern, and the Western, or Red Sea of modern times.

紅夷 Hung-i, savage tribes, clad with cotton sashes and red turbans, living between Yun-nan and Annam. They trade with the Annamites, bartering precious stones for salt, which they are said to be without.

虹口 Hung k'au, or Hong-que, the site of the American settlement in Shanghai. This is situated on the Wusung river, at the point of junction with the Hwang-pu, on which the British and French settlements are situated.

紅毛 Hung-mau, a name given to the Dutch, on coming to Canton, and then extended to all foreigners. In Asiatic Russia the English are called "*Khundi*," or "Red heads." See Hung-t'u-sü.

紅帽回子 Hung-mau hwui-tsz', the Mohammedan Turkmans wearing "red (fez) caps." They came from Persia, and from countries beyond the Caspian. The first Jews coming to China, also came viâ Persia, and were called "Blue-cap" hwui tsz'.

橫濱 Hung-pin, the port of Yokohama in Japan.

紅頭嶼 Hung-t'u-sü, the Bashee islands, to the S. of Formosa, belonging to Spain. The name "red headed islets," denotes their barbarian tenure. They are also called Botel Tobago.

華夏 Hwa-hia, China. See Chung hwa.

花旗國 Hwa-k'i kwoh, the "Country of the flowery flag." A Chinese popular name for the United States, not now used in formal documents. See Mei kwoh.

淮南 Hwai-nan, the name of an ancient circuit, including most of the old province of Yang chau.

琿春城 Hwan-chun ching, a garrison post near the coast, in the S.E. part of Kirin, not far from the Corean frontier. It is subordinate to Ninguta, the largest town, but not the capital of Kirin. The district round is very extensive, but is inhabited only by fishermen and hunters.

13

黄支國 Hwang-chi kwoh, a portion of Cochin China. Rhinoceroses were sent from this country as tribute to the Chinese emperor P'ing-ti, of the Han dynasty.

黄海 Hwang hai. This is a doubtful name met with in later Chinese composition and referred to the Tung yang, or Yellow Sea. This was anciently called the 渤海, Puh-hai, being the point at which in the time of Yü the 逆河, Nih-ho, formed by the conjunction of the nine streams of the Ho, or Hwang Ho, poured its waters into the "turbid sea." -

黄河 Hwang ho, the Hoang ho, or the Yellow River. This name may have been derived from its turbidity, imparted by the clayey soil of the Great Plain, through which it runs. In this respect the Yangtsz' might vie with the Hwang ho for muddiness. It is referred by some to the relation of the yellow or imperial colour to the central point of the Chinese planisphere, representing the "middle kingdom." The Hwang-ho, in keeping with the expression 河爲中國患遠矣, was called Kara mouran, the "Black river," by the Mongols, or the Caramoran of Marco Polo. See Ta c'huen.

黄旗國 Hwang-k'i kwoh, the "Country of the Yellow Flag," a name given to the kingdom of Denmark, from the accidental colour of the flags of Danish ships.

皇國 Hwang kwoh, a name given by the Japanese to their country, as ruled by a theocratic dynasty. See Shin kwoh.

黄埔 Hwang-pu, or Whampoa, the anchorage for foreign ships, distant some twelve miles from Canton.

黄浦 Hwang-p'u, or Wongpoo, the tidal channel or river, upon which the native city of Shanghai is situated. It penetrates for some forty miles into the interior, and helps to drain the complicated network of inland lakes.

忽必烈 Hwuh-pieh-lieh, Kublai Khan, sometimes called Kilawan Hwuhpihlieh, founder of the Mongolian dynasty of China. He was the son of Tuli, fourth son of Temngin or Genghis Khan.

忽魯謨斯 Hwuh-lu-mu-sz', the city of Ormus, or Hormaz, in the Persian Gulf.

回城八 Hwui-ching-pah, the eight (or more) Mohammedan cities of Eastern or Chinese Turkestan, inhabited by Turkish and other tribes. The old tribe of the Kara Kitai, under the name of the Kara Kaitach, is found in these cities.

輝發 Hwui-fah, or Hœifan hotun in Kirin, a small garrisoned post, lying on a branch of the Songari, S.S.E. of Kirin ula, and under its jurisdiction.

回黑 Hwui-heh, the Uigurs, a Turkic tribe, from which the Usbeks are in part descended. They were connected with the Kau-ché, and founded a kingdom in Turfan, or Tangut, called Kau-chung. The word Uigur is applied to Tangut by the Mongolian historians. There were On-Uigurs and Tokus Uigurs.

回回 Hwui-hwui, or 回子, Hwui-tsz', the Persian Mohammedans, Uigurs, Tajiks, and other Turkic or Iranic followers of Mahomet, in and near China. The character is sometimes offensively written 狆回. The earliest period of their arrival in any number in China, was during the domination of the Liau, Kin and Yuen dynasties of Tungusic and Mongolic sovereigns. Their name is evidently derived from that of the Uigurs. Uigur is a term common to the Mongolian dialects, and signifies "a stranger." The Chinese word

14

hwui supports this meaning.

回 紇 Hwui-k'i, Turkic tribes, to the number of fifteen, descended from Hiung-nu. Diamonds, or the corundum, are said to have come to China from these tribes.

會 稽 Hwui-k'i, a name of Kiangnan.

回 疆 Hwui-kiang, a name of Chinese Turkestan. See Sin-kiang.

回 鶻 Hwui-kuh, the Uigurs. See Hwui-heh.

惠 寧 城 Hwui-ning ching, one of the garrisons, N.E. of, and attached to Kuldja, or Hwui-yuen.

回 部 Hwui-pu, Mohammedan tribes.

輝 特 部 Hwui-teh pu, or Khoits, a tribe of Mongols, living west of Si-ning, not far from the Azure Sea, and arranged under one standard.

惠 遠 城 Hwui-yuen ching, the capital city of I'li, in Lat. 43° 36' N., and Long. 82° 30' E. This city, called by the natives, *Kura*, and by the Russians, *Guldschu* or *Kuldja*, lies on the N. bank of the I'li river, which runs into Lake Balkash. It contains some 50,000 people, and carries on considerable trade with adjacent districts. It was built by Kien-lung, but is now lost to China, with all the surrounding country. Coal is found in the district.

I

夷 I', the name of the barbarian tribes, "Great bowmen," on the E. of the Chinese kingdom of the beginning of the Chau dynasty. They occupied Shantung, the coast-line to the S. of the Hwai river, and a great portion of what is now Kiangsu and Nganhwui. They merged into the *man* of the S. All these terms are used very promiscuously. The term I' was formerly applied offensively to foreigners, but is now expressly forbidden in the treaties. The I' were described as having nine divisions.

宜 昌 I-chang, a prefectural city in Hupeh, situated on the left bank of the Yangtsz', distant from Peking 3,540 *li*, and 360 geographical miles from Hankow. It is in Lat. 30° 49' N., and Long. 111° 10' 20" E. and has seven districts attached to it. It is sometimes called I-ling, and is nearly 1,100 statute miles from the mouth of the Yangtsz'.

義 州 I-chau, in Shingking, department of Kinchau fu, 4Lat. 1° 30' N., and Long. 121° 20' E.

義 州 城 I-chau ching, a garrison subordinate to Shingking pun ching. It is near one of the gates in the Palisade, and is under the jurisdiction of the Manchu general at Moukden. This sub-department was formerly known as 同 昌, T'ung-chang.

儀 眞 I'-chin, an old name of I-ching hien, in Yangchau fu. See Chin chau.

伊 克 昭 明 I-keh-chau ming, one of the six corps of Inner Mongolia, living on the Yellow River, beyond the Great Wall, and N. of Kansuh.

伊 澗 I-kien, a name of Lohyang, in Honan, an ancient capital.

伊犂 I'-li, a name derived from the river I'-li, and given by the Chinese to an immense tract of country, nearly as large as Mongolia. It is inhabited by various tribes, and was divided into two *lu*, or "circuits," by their relation to the T'ien Shan. The *Peh Luh*, or Northern Circuit, comprised ancient Songaria, except Urumtsi and Barkul, attached to Kansuh. The *Nan Lu*, is called Eastern or Chinese Turkestan. The whole country is more or less under independent Mohammedan rule.

彝陵 I'-ling, the official name of I-chang. There is a district city in Hunan, named *I-chang hien*, to be carefully distinguished from I-chang fu, in Hupeh.

依耐國 I-nai kwoh, an ancient name of Yingeshar. See Ying-kih-sha-rh.

意大理亞 I'-ta-li-ya, a name given to Italy in Chinese books, as the country of Matteo Ricci.

伊吾盧 I-wu-lu, an ancient name of Hamil, a town in Barkul, on the confines of Kansuh. See Há-mih. The country around this present settlement was held, during the Han period, by military colonists. In the time of the After Wei it was first erected into the I-wu-kiun.

J

柔佛 Jau-fuh, Johore, a state in the S. of the Malayan Peninsula. The chief town, on a small river, all of the same name, was formerly a place of considerable trade.

柔國 Jau kwoh, an ancient principality on the coast of Shantung. It is said in the Annals of the Eastern Han, to have belonged to 瑯琊郡, Lang-ya kiun, the present 沂州府, Ni-chau fu.

熱河 Jeh-ho, or Jehol, "Warm Stream," the name of a stream flowing from Chahar into the Gulf of Pehchihli. There is a summer residence of the emperors of China near it, lying to the N.E. of Peking, or 170 miles due N. of Taku in Lat. 41° 4′ N., and Long. 117° 50′ E. See Pí-shú-shan-chwang. The district is in Ching-teh fu.

日喝則 Jeh-hoh-tseh, a place or district in Ulterior Thibet, possibly identical with Zhi-kátsé, or Teshu h'lumbu. See Chah-shih-lun-pu ching.

日南 Jeh-nan, an ancient name of Cochin China or some other adjoining state. This is perhaps identical with Lin-yih, and the Siang kiun of the Ts'in dynasty.

日本 Jeh-pun, Nippon, or Japan, the "Dayspring." See Shin kwoh. This name dates, in Chinese writings, from the T'ang period.

日本國 Jeh-pun kwoh, the "Country of the rising sun," the Chinese original of Sypangu, Marco Polo's name for Japan. But for the glowing account of *Cathay* and *Sypangu*, given by the Venetian traveller, Columbus would probably never have been urged to the discovery of the western world.

冉駹 Jen-p'ang, the name of certain tribes on the W. of ancient China Proper. They inhabited the country which is now included in the present sub-department of Mau chau (Sech'uen), with Kokonor, or Ts'ing-hai on its western border.

蝡 蠕 Ju-ju, or Yuen-yuen. This name is very variously written and sounded in Chinese works. It refers to a Turkic tribe of Hiung-nu, or Huns as they are sometimes called. During the Ts'in dynasty they made an inroad upon China. They were formerly called Jen-fei, or Jau-jen, according to some Chinese authors.

如 來 佛 Ju-lai-fuh, the name of the Buddha of the present calpa, Tathagata.

如 利 亞 Ju-li-ya, the Japanese name for Syria, and the Nestorian faith. The Syrians and the Nestorian faith were known to the Chinese by the name of *Ta-ts'in*.

如 德 亞 Ju-teh-ya, the name for Syria and Palestine (Judæa) in Chinese and Japanese works. See T'ien chuh kwoh. This name seems much more homophonous than the 猶 太 國, Yu-t'ai kwoh of the Christian translators.

嗕 Juh, Ugro-tataric tribes, allied to the *Kiang*. See San miau.

戎 Jung, the mounted barbarians of the W. from whom came the Ts'inites, founders of the Ts'in dynasty.

娀 Jung, an ancient state, near the Kwanlun range in Thibet. *Sheah*, the reputed author of the invention of writing, was born here, his mother being the daughter of its chief.

絨 轄 城 Jung-hiah ching, or Jounghia, a town and district of Ulterior Thibet, between Ghieding and Niclam, in the S.

戎 狄 Jung-tih, tribes in Turfan, armed and mounted in chariots. This term was also loosely applied to all the barbarian tribes of Yü's time.

K

蓋 州 城 Kai chau ching, a port in Shingking, possessing an excellent harbour, in Lat. 40° 30' E., and Long. 122° 30' E.

開 封 府 K'ai-fung fu, the chief city of Honan province, probably identical with the Chin of Fuh-hi, and formerly the capital of the state of Wei, and of the whole empire in A.D. 960 under the Sung dynasty. Its name has been often changed, since the third century, but it has kept its present designation since the Ming period. Here in A.D. 1163, a Jewish synagogue was erected, by permission of the emperor Hiau-tsung.

開 平 K'ai-p'ing, or Shang-tu, one of the capitals of the Mongols in the 14th century. Lat. 42° 25' N., and Long. 116° E. distant from Peking 700 *li*, and called *Clemein fu* by Marco Polo. It was the same place as Siuen-teh, or as Wan-ts'iuen-tu of the next (Ming) dynasty.

蓋 平 縣 Kai-p'ing hien, in Shingking. It is a district town in Fung-t'ien fu.

開 原 城 K'ai-yuen ching, subordinate to Shingking pun ching, in Lat. 42° 40' N., and Long. 123° 15' E. The 上 京, Shangking of the Kin dynasty was near this place.

開 原 縣 K'ai-yuen hien, a district town in Fung-t'ien fu, in Shingking. This was anciently called 肅 愼 地, Suh-shin-ti, as a seat of the Nu-chin or

澉 浦 Kan-pu, or Canfu, the ancient port of Hangchow, visited by the Arabians in the 9th century, and by Marco Polo. It is now washed away, or submerged. It was situated in what is now called Hai-yen hien, and was at the mouth of the middle entrance of the Yangtsz', now closed. See Cha-pu.

康 Kang, Kham, or Khamba, a name given to the eastern part of Anterior Thibet, lying on the confines of Kokonor and Sechuen. See Keh-muh.

耿 Kang, the name of the capital of the empire of the Shang period, answering to the present **吉 州**, Kih chau, in P'ing-yang fu (Shansi). This was the fourth capital of these changeable monarchs. See Siang.

耿 州 Kang chau, an old name of Kih chau (Shansi), identical with **耿**, Kang, which see.

岡 腸 Kang-hoh, a branch of the head waters of the Indus, in Thibet, sometimes confounded with the Ganges river, but properly called the *Ganga*, not *Gunga*.

康 居 Kang-ku, the ancient name of Shoghnan, or Sogdiana in Independent Tartary, in-habited by the Sacai, a wild race. It was called Kang kwoh during the T'ang dynasty, when, as well as in the Sui time, the people of the country were great rovers.

高 昌 Kau-chang, the country of the Uigurs, identified with Turfan, or Tangut. It was des-troyed A.D. 640. In the *Nan Shi* (**南 史**), *Li-yen shou*, who died about A.D. 670, speaks of a plant growing in this country, which yields a fine thread called *Peh-tieh* (**白 疊**), used in making soft and white cloth. See Ho-si and Ho-tien ching.

高 車 Kau-ché, the Ugro-tataric tribes from whom the Usbeks are descended. They gave their name to Kau-chang, the country of the Uigurs, with whom they amalgamated. In some cases the Uigurs would seem to be included under this term of Kau-ché or Chui-che.

高 附 國 Kau-fu kwoh, an extensive country to the S.W. of the Massagetæ, the Indo-Scy-thians of western historians.

高 句 驪 Kau-k'u-li, a country in Liautung, now called *Ku-yung hien*.

橐 離 國 Kau-li kwoh, the country of Corea, as formerly written.

高 麗 國 Kau-li kwoh, the name in common use for Corea, derived from that of a usurper, more especially employed in connection with the drug Ginseng. It is divided into eight provinces or *tau*. See Cháu-sien and Kau shi.

口 北 道 K'au-peh tau, an extensive region in northeastern Chihli, beyond the Great Wall, with Tolonnor for its chief town.

高 氏 Kau shi, the name of a man who usurped the kingdom of Corea, during the Han dy-nasty, and named it after himself.

高 失 踏 Kau-shih-tah, the Coromandel coast.

鈎 叮 Kau-ting, the kingdom of *Caraian* of Marco Polo, near the present Yunnan.

蒿 齊 特 Kau-tsí-teh, Khaotchit, or Haochit, a tribe of Mongols, living near the S.W. spur of the Inner Hing-ngan mountains.

客 家 Keh-kia, or Hakka, "settlers" from Kia-ying chau, who arrived in the Canton pro-vince about the time of the Yuen dynasty. As they are called "foreigners" in Kia-ying, they must have migrated from some other district. It is probable that this agricultural tribe came from Kiangsi province. Their dialect is related to the southern mandarin, but is apparently an older form of it, intermediate between the Punti and the mandarin.

喀喇沁 K'eh-lah-chin, the Kartsin, or Kharachin, a tribe of Mongols, living W. of Tsakhar, just beyond the Great Wall.

喀喇喀沙 K'eh-lah-k'eh-sha, the Karakash, the *Sarikhia* of Moorcroft, a river in Khoten, which joins the Sujet. It is in the bed of this river, when nearly dried up, that nephrite, or jade, so highly esteemed by the Chinese, is found. The town of the same name is ten miles to the W. of Ilchí, or Khoten, and near it there are numerous hot springs, with a temperature from 70° to 130° Fah. Salt is abundant in the surrounding district.

喀喇沙爾城 K'eh-lah-sha-rh ching, Kharashar, or Harashar, the principal town and garrison in the southern circuit of I'li. It lies in Lat. 42° 15′ N., and Long. 87° 05′ E. near lake Bostang. The district connected with it is very extensive.

喀木 K'eh-muh, Kham. See Kang.

喀爾喀 K'eh-rh-k'eh, the Kalkas, the richest and, after the Tsakhars, the most numerous of the Mongol tribes, inhabiting Outer Mongolia. They are divided into four khanates, or eighty standards. Each of these Khans claims direct descent from Genghis Khan.

喀爾喀扎薩克圖汗部 K'eh-rh-k'eh-Chah-sah-keh Han-pú, the Kalkas of the Dzassaktú Khanate. This is the smallest of the four khanates, and lies S. of Uliasutai, reaching to Cobdo and Barkul, on the W. and S. There are many lakes in its limits.

喀爾喀車臣汗部 K'eh-rh-k'eh Ché-chin Han-pu, the Kalkas of the Tsetsen Khanate, lying W. of Hurunpir, with the Tuchetu Khanate on the W., and extending from Russia on the N. to Inner Mongolia on the S.

喀爾喀部 K'eh-rh-k'eh pu, the Kalkas who inhabit parts of Kokonor. They are but few compared with those in Outer Mongolia.

喀爾喀三音諾顏部 K'eh-rh-k'eh San-yin noh-yen pú, the Kalkas of San-noin. This khanate lies W. of the Tuchetu Khanate, N. of Gobi, and S. of the territory of Uliasutai and the Ulianghai tribes.

喀爾喀土謝圖汗部 K'eh-rh-k'eh Tu-sié-tu Han-pú, the Kalkas of the Tuchetu Khanate. This khanate is central with respect to the other three Kalkan khanates of Outer Mongolia, and is the largest and most important of them all. The road from Kiakhta to Kalgan lies within its borders.

喀什葛爾城 K'eh-shih-kieh-rh ching, Kashgar in Chinese Turkestan, about 1,000 *li* W. from Aksu, situated on a river of the same name, in Lat. 39° 25′ N., and Long. 74° E. This large town, the capital of the dominions of Yakoob Beg, the ruler of Chinese Turkestan, contains nearly 100,000 inhabitants from all parts of Central Asia. From the meeting of four great caravan-roads at this point, it must always be a great commercial emporium. Russia has invited the Khan of Kokand to attack Yakoob Beg, who by his defeat of the revolting Mahommedan tribes in 1865, became master of what had been Chinese territory since A.D. 1750. Fort Vernöe, a large Russian military colony on the N. of the lake Issu-kul, is only 400 miles from Kashgar. The Kashgari, Khokani, Khoteni and Yarkandi are dialects of the Turki language. See Su-lch kwoh.

克西克騰 Keh-si-keh-tang, or Keckikten, a tribe of Mongols living 570 *li* N.E. of Kaupeh tau.

肯 特 山 Ken-teh shan, the Kentei mountains, a spur of the northern branch of the Altai range, called by the Russians, the Daourian mountains. Here the Sagalien river takes its rise.

旗 K'i, the Tartar bannermen. See Pah k'i.

冀 州 K'i chau, a division of China, in Yü's time, including part of Shansi and Pehchihli, with the three departments of Chang-teh, Wei-hwui and Hwaiking in Honan, and the western portion of Shingking, or Liautung. These nine regions had been similarly named by Chuen hiuh.

跂 踵 戎 Ki-chung jung, a "club-footed" tribe from beyond Shamoh.

雞 籠 Ki-lung, or Kelung, a coaling-port in the N. of Formosa.

罽 賓 國 Ki-pin kwoh, Cophené, a part of Afghanistan, whose capital is said to be 12,200 li from Si-ngan fu. In some Chinese works this is said to be Samarcand.

契 丹 K'i-tan, or Kitai, the name of the Tungusic progenitors of the Liau dynasty, under the T'ang, called also Sien-pi. They gave their name to China as Kitai, Catai, or Cathay. Dr. Oppert asserts the Mongolic origin of these Kara Kitai. See Hiau-lo-ko-muh-li.

迦 古 羅 國 Kia-ku-lo kwoh, a country in India, the reputed source of several drugs.

加 蘭 丹 Kia-lan-tan, Kih-lan-tan, or Kalantan, a small state on the E. coast of the Malay Peninsula, tributary to Siam. It formerly sent joint tribute to China of ebony, cloves and pepper.

咖 嚼 巴 Kia-liu-pa, Batavia, or Java. See Koh-lah-pa.

加 羅 布 Kia-lo-pu, a place in the China Sea. The description points to the most southerly part of Cambodia.

伽 陂 羅 Kia-po-lo, the birthplace of Sakyamuni, near Goruckpore.

加 濕 彌 羅 Kia-shih-mi-lo, the country of Cashmere, the Capatyrus of the ancients. It is sometimes called Ko-shih-mih, unless this be the name of a country to the north of Cashmere.

加 闍 那 國 Kia-tu-la kwoh, a country placed N. of India, near Cashmere, and the reputed source of the best assafœtida.

嘉 峪 關 Kia-yu-kwan, the most westerly gate in the Great Wall, at the end of it, between Ngansi fu and Suh-chau in Kansuh. K'i-pin kwoh is said to be 9,000 li beyond this pass.

羌 Kiang, Ugro-tataric tribes in Tangut. See Si-kiang and Juh. This name is given as a designation of the San miau, which see.

江 浙 Kiang-cheh, a name of Chekiang in the Mongolian period.

江 戶 Kiang-hu, Yeddo in Japan, the "River's door."

江 淮 Kiang-hwai, a name of Nganhwui and Kiangnan.

江 口 Kiang-k'au, the "river's mouth," a name erroneously assigned in European maps to the river Yangtsz'.

江 敏 城 Kiang-min ching, a town and district in Anterior Thibet, S.W. of H'lassa, and near T'eshu lumbu.

江 南 Kiang-nan, a name loosely applied to the country around Nanking, or to Nganhwui, and Kiangsu. The name was originally given to all those departments of Nganhwui and Kiang su, which lay S. of the Kiang, or Yangtsz' River. There was also a division of this district into *Kiangnan tung tau*, answering to Kiangnan and Chekiang, and *Kiangnan si tau*, including much of Kiangsi, which may have derived its name from this old division.

江寧 Kiang-ning, Nanking, as named by the present dynasty. See Kin-ling. This name had formerly been given to Nanking by the T'ang dynasty.

江北 Kiang-peh, the name given to a district including all those departments of Nganhwui and Kiangsu, lying N. of the Yang-tsz'-kiang. These departments were also distinguished by the terms *shang* and *shia*, according as they lay "up," or "down" the river. These still obtain among natives of the provinces.

江舌 Kiang-sheh, a name of the island of Tsung Ming, at the mouth of the Yangtsz'-kiang.

姜水 Kiang-shwui, an ancient name of the Yangtsz'-kiang, or the Blackwater, in Kokonor or Kansuh.

江達城 Kiang-tah ching, the town and district of Kiangta, in Thibet, between H'lassa and H'lari.

江東 Kiang-tung, the right bank of the river Yangtsz', in its course through Hupeh. This name is also applied to Suchau, as an abbreviation of Kiang-nan-tung-tau.

交州府 Kiau-chau fu, or Hué, the capital of Annam, or Cochin China, situated on a small river of the same name.

交阯 Kiau-chí, or 交趾, a cynical name given to the Cochin Chinese, because like some of the Japanese, their men and women were said to bathe together publicly. See Nan-chí'au-chí-ti.

教門 Kiau-men, the Mohammedan sect. See Hwui-hwui.

嶠南 Kiau-nan, an old name of Kwangsi *province*.

膠東 Kiau-tung, the present P'ing-tu chau in Shantung province.

結定城 Kieh-ting ching, Ghieding, or Dingghie, a town and district of Ulterior Thibet, S. of Teshu-hl'umbu.

建康 Kien-kang, the name of Nanking, as the capital of the Eastern Tsin dynasty, which altered the old name of Kien-yeh, given to Nanking by the Wu dynasty.

建國 Kien kwoh, the kingdom of Fukien, the *Chonka* of Marco Polo. See Min.

建陵 Kien-ling, an old name of Kweiliu fu (Kwangsi).

虔那 Kien-na, a country to the S.W. of China, visited by Ta Hi-tung, in A.D. 674.

劍南 Kien-nan, a name of one of the large divisions of China in the T'ang time, called *tau*. It included parts of Sech'uen and Kweichau, and was divided into east and west portions.

黔首 K'ien-shau, the "Black-heads," a name given to the Chinese by Chí Hwang Tí, from their black turbans.

黔地 K'ien-ti, a name of Kweichau province. This is said to be the country near 蠻方, Man-fang, the neighbourhood of the Man-tsz'. See Ta-wan-kuh-loh.

虔土羅 K'ien-t'u-lo, Candahar, in Afghanistan.

建業 Kien-yeh, a name of the city of Nanking, as the later capital of the empire of the rulers of Wu. See King-ling. Chinese writers refer this name to Shang-yuen hien, the premier district of Kiang-ning fu (Kiangsu). See Lung-shau-shan.

乞 伏 K'ih-fuh, a division of the Sien-pí, living to the W. of Shensi of the present time.

吉 林 Kih-lin, Kirin, or Ghirin, a large country to the N.E. of Shingking, bordering on the Sea of Japan, and the Gulf of Tartary. It is bounded on the N. by the *Hing Ngan Ling*, or Daourian Mountains, E. and N.E. by the ocean, S.E. by Corea, and the Palisade which divides it from Shingking, and W. by Mongolia and Tsitsihar. It is divided into three *ting* departments, namely, Kirin ula, Petuné ula, and Changch'un. This extensive region is thinly peopled by Manchus, who live by fishing and hunting.

激 國 Kih-kwoh, a country to the S. of Fu-nan, whose people, the Hwan-t'ien, usurped the Kingdom of Fu-nan.

吉 林 城 Kih-lin ching, Kirin ula, the principal town of Kirin, in Lat. 43° 45′ N., and Long. 26° 25′ E. It is situated on the Songari river, and is a poor-looking place for the capital of a province, consisting of a few houses for the officers and staff, and a collection of huts.

吉 林 理 事 廳 Kih-lin li-sz' ting, Kirin ula hotun, the name of the commandery of Kirin, indicating that it has the control of the whole province.

吉 里 門 Kih-li-men, the Carimon islands, a little to the W. of Java, infested by Malay pirates.

吉 俻 Kih-pí, Kibi, the reputed inventor of the Japanese *Katakana* character. He visited China in A.D. 733. See Hung-fah.

吉 礁 Kih-tsah, Quedah near Penang, in the Malay peninsula.

金 州 城 Kin-chau ching, in Shingking, subordinate to the head garrison, is the port of Moukden, and distant from it 15 leagues. The harbour is rapidly silting up.

錦 州 府 Kin-chau fu, a department in Shingking, lying along the gulf of Liautung. It is divided into two *chau* districts, *Ningyuen* and *I'*, and two *hien* districts, *Kin* and *Kwang-ning*, each having a small garrisoned town. See Liau-si.

金 齒 Kin-ch'i, Laos tribes near the *Lan-tsang* river, who gilded their teeth. Their country was the *Zardandan* of Marco Polo.

金 川 Kin chuen, the name of a river rising in Kokonor, and of a district for which see Ta Kin chuen.

錦 縣 Kin hien, a district of Kin-chau fu in Shingking. The town is in Lat. 41° 06′. N., and Long. 121° 18′ E.

金 陵 Kin-ling, the "Golden mounds," one of the oldest names of Nanking. It had been called *Moh-ling* by T'sin Chi-hwang. Little remains of the beauty with which *Hungwu* the founder of the Ming dynasty adorned his capital, but some colossal statues which ornamented the imperial mausolea.

金 門 Kin-mon, the island of Quemoy, a little to the E. of Amoy island.

金 山 Kin-shan, the Altai mountains, running between Lat. 50° and 52° 30′ N. This name "Golden mountain" has been given to California. The emperor of the Kin Tartars was called Altan Khan, the Golden Khan.

金 沙 江 Kin-sha-kiang, the name of the Upper Yang-tsz' before its junction with the

Min river. The department of Ting-chau fu in Fukien, was formerly called Kin-sha.

金臺 Kin-t'ai, an old name of Pehchihli province.

董子國 Kin-tsz' kwoh, situated on the E. of Ningpo fu, and said to have yielded tin in former days.

荆州 King-chau, the province of Yü corresponding to *Hu-kwang* of later date, very nearly.

京兆 King-cháu, a name of Si-ngan fu in Shensi, under the Han. See King chau fu.

京兆府 King-chau fu, an old name of Si-ngan fu, in Shensi, under the *Kin* sovereigns in A.D. 1142. It was also known as Chang-ngan and Hien-yang.

京畿道 King-ki-tau, the name of the capital, and of the metropolitan *tau*, or province, of Corea. The first character was attempted to be changed by the Chinese, as they claimed that there could be but one *King*, the residence of the Suzerain. This is also one of the names of the metropolitan district of Peking, as one of the 15 *tau* into which the empire was divided in the reign of *Yuen-tsung* of the T'ang dynasty. This division is still retained in the *Tsin Shin Shu*, the "Red Book," issued regularly as an official Court Guide.

硯伽 King-kia, the Gunga, the Ganges of India. See Hang ho.

荆江 King kiang, the Ta Kiang or Yangtsz', from *King-ho k'au*, the point of junction of the stream which is the outlet of the T'ung-ting lake, with the main stream (Upper Yangtsz'), as far as the city of *King-chau fu*.

景教 King kian, the "illustrious religion," of the Nestorians. See T'ien-chuh kiau.

京師 King-sz', or Kinsai, the name of *Hangchau*, as the capital of the Sung dynasty, in the time of Marco Polo. The Chinese characters denote the capital of the empire, as the residence of the sovereign, wherever that may be. Peking is accordingly so named upon native maps and in official books. See Shau-shan or Shau-shen.

慶綏城 King-shu ching, the chief town of the intendancy of *Kurkwa usu*.

京塘 King-t'ang, or 京提塘, King-t'i-t'ang, the Chinese Postmaster General in Peking, under the Board of War. There are two such officers in each province, called 省提塘, Sang-t'i-t'ang, regulating roads and bunds.

景德鎮 King-teh-chin, the chief town of the "Potteries" in Kiangsi, and one of the five great marts of China. See Wu-chin.

京都 King-tu, Kioto, or Miaco, the residential city of the Mikado of Japan.

九州 Kiu-chau, the "Nine regions" of China, as divided, or adopted from Chuen Hiuh, by the Great Yü. The term is still used in composition. These regions or provinces had been increased to twelve by Shun.

九眞 Kiu-chin, or Kowchin (Cochin?), a name of Annam and Cambodia, as forming part of China. See Siang kiun. There is a 九眞山, in Hanyang hien, opposite to the Ta Kiun Shan, near the Yangtsz' river.

九江 Kiu-kiang. This name was anciently applied to the T'ungting lake in Hunan, but is now the name of one of the treaty ports, *Kiukiang fu*.

舊教 Kiu-kiau, the "ancient faith," or the Jewish religion. See Tau-kin-kiau.

九龍 Kiu-lung, the sub-district of Kowloong, opposite Hongkong, which has been partly ceded to the British crown.

九龍江 Kiu-lung kiang, the Meikong or Camboja river. See Nan-chang kiang.

九塞 Kiu-seh, the nine frontier-forts of the old empire of China, to which Ts'in Chi-hwang added another the 紫塞 Tsz'-seh or "Red rampart," the Great Wall of China. These nine defences were as follows,—太汾, T'ai-fan (Shansi),—句注, Ku-chu, at 鴈門, Yen-men, the 代州, Tai-chau (Shansi) of the present day,—澠阨, Min-ngeh, and 殽阪, Hiau-fan, in 宏農, Hung-nung, a name of the present 陝州, Shen-chau (Honan),—荊阮 King-yuen and 方城 Fang-ching in 楚, T'su, or Hukwang,—井陘, Tsing-ying, in Ta-t'ung fu (Shansi),—居庸 Ku-yung, in Siuen-hua fu (Pehchihli), and 令疵 Ling-tsz' in Liau-si (Shingking). This word 塞, Seh was formerly pronounced as 賽, Sai, a common Mohammedan surname, and has the meaning of 寨, Chai, a stockade, or military encampment.

九癭 Kiu-ying, a race of wizened cretins, dwelling in mountainous regions beyond the desert of Gobi. Their goitres are distinctly referred by Chinese writers to the character of the water of the district. See Wu-shan-kiah.

捐毒 Kiuen-tuh, a name of India and Syria. See T'ien-tuh.

瓊州 Kiung-chau, the northern part of the island of Hainan.

哥老 Ko-lau, the name and watchword of a secret society of disbanded soldiers in Hunan and other provinces.

噶喇巴 Koh-lah-pa, Batavia, or the whole island of Java, as it is usually known to the Chinese, from the native name Kalapa, for the cocoanut. They often write it without the two first characters, as Pa (巴).

覺羅 Koh-lo, the Ghioro, or the "Golden race," the surname of the Manchu reigning family. See Ta Kin. The imperial kindred is spoken of as the Tsung-shih koh-lo. They were also distinguished by their single-peaked shoes, now worn by officials generally.

郭爾喀 Koh-rh-keh, the Ghoorkas of Nepaul. See Ni-p'o-lo.

郭爾羅斯 Koh-rh-lo-sz', a tribe of Mongols, the Khorlos, on the N.W. of Shingking.

噶達素齊老山 Koh-tah-sú-tsí-lau shan, a lofty peak in Lat. 35° N., and Long. 95° E. near which the Alotan ho, a source of the Yellow River, rises.

戈壁 Ko-pih, or 大戈壁, Ta Kopih, the Great Desert of Cobi or Gobi, called also Shamoh, Hanhai and Taklan Makan. It extends from the eastern frontier of Mongolia, southwestward to the further frontier of Turkestan, to within six miles of Ilchí, the chief town of Khoten. It thus comprises some twenty-three degrees of longitude in length, and from three to ten degrees of latitude in breadth, being about 2,100 miles in its greatest length. In some places it is arable. Some idea may be formed of the terror with which this "Sea of Sand," with its vast billows of shifting sands is regarded, by the legend that in one of the storms, 360 cities were all buried in the space of twenty-four hours. Gold coins of great weight, and other articles, are said to have been found in certain lofty hillocks, on the edge of the desert. This attests to the wealth of the surrounding country, of which Herodotus in his account of the desert in which gold dust was thrown up by ants, seems to have had some notion. See Liu-sha, and Lo-to-keh ching.

科布多城 Ko-pu-to ching, Khobdo, or Cobdo, lies in the N.W. of Mongolia. It is bounded N. and W. by Russia, N.E. by Ulianghai, S.E. by the Dzassaktu Khanate, S. by Barkul, a nominal part of Kansuh, and W. by Tarbagatai. Cobdo comprises eleven tribes of Kalkas, divided into thirty-one standards, garrisoned by the *amban*, who resides at a city of the same name. The amban is subordinate to the resident at Uliasutai. The garrisoned city is situated on a branch of the river of the same name, which runs into one of the many lakes of this province. It carries on some trade with Urga, and is situated in Lat. 47° 30′ N., and Long. 85° 30′ E.

科 爾 沁 Ko-rh-chin, the Kortchins, a large tribe of Mongols occupying the country S. and W. of the valley of the river Nonni, in the province of Tsitsihar, on the confines of Kirin. Tin is brought from their territory.

庫 車 城 Ku-ché ching, formerly the name of a district state, but now usually applied to a large garrisoned town, called the gate of Chinese, or Eastern Turkestan. It lies about 100 miles W. of Bukur, in Lat. 41° 37′ N., and Long. 82° 55′ E. on the W. of Harashar, at the S. of the T'ien Shan. The surrounding district is cultivated, and some trade in linen, sal ammoniac, cinnabar, quicksilver, copper, sulphur and saltpetre is carried on. See Kweitsz' kwoh.

古 格 Ku-keh, Gugé, a part of N'ari, in Thibet, consisting of two valleys.

巨 港 Kü-kiang, Palembang, formerly an independent kingdom of Sumatra, and having a large trade in pepper and tin from the island of Banca. It is sometimes identified with *San-fuh-tsi*. The name, with a change of the first character, is sometimes given to Jambi, a little N. of Palembang.

庫 可 諾 爾 K'u-ko-noh-rh, Koko nor, the "Blue lake" country. See T'sing hai.

俱 藍 Kü-lan, the town of Coulan, or Quilon, the capital of the state of Travancore, in Lat. 8° 55′ N., and Long. 76° 45′ E.

鼓 浪 嶼 Ku-lang-su, the island of Kulangsu, near Amoy.

咕 嘞 Ku-leh, the Koran.

古 里 Ku-li, Calicut, or Calli, or Calliana in Malabar, a vast centre of commerce in ancient time, and the port of departure for travellers to and from China. This may have been the *Cattigara* of Ptolemy, which has been variously referred to Canton or Cambodia.

古 俚 國 Ku-li kwoh, the country of Malabar. A place called *Hwuh-lu-ma*, or *Hwuh-lu-mu*, has been variously referred to this coast, to Quilon, and to Hormaz in the Persian Gulf.

古 里 班 卒 Ku-li-pan-tsuh, Masulipatam, a port in the Madras Presidency, one of the best harbours on the whole coast. It formed a part of the first acquisition of extensive territory from the Nizam, by the East India Company. The fame of its chintzes and calicoes had created a demand in Persia and China, to which latter country it was brought as tribute, more especially from Siam. The fame of the goods, and some of the names of the fabrics of the East India Company were hereditarily derived from these cotton goods brought from Siam, Malacca and other places.

庫 倫 K'u-lun, Kurun, or Urga, a large town in the Tuchetu Khanate, where the high-priest, called *Kukuktu* resides, ruling over the Kalkas of Mongolia. It lies in Lat. 48° 20′ N., and Long. 107° 30′ E. on the Tola river, a branch of the Selenga, and is one of the stations of

Grant's Trans-Mongolian Telegraph.

鉅 鹿 Ku-luh, a prefecture of Ts'in Chi-hwang, in Pehchihli, answering to a part of Shun-teh fu, still bearing this name.

古 麻 剌 Ku-ma-lah, Trincomalee in Ceylon. This may refer to Coulan in Travancore, which rejoices in the profusion of some eight or ten aliases in various languages.

姑 墨 國 Ku-meh kwoh, a place on the borders of Khoten.

古 北 口 Ku-peh k'au, a pass in the Great Wall, in Lat. 40° 43′ N.

庫 爾 喀 喇 烏 蘇 城 Ku-rh-k'eh-lah Wu-su ching, or the garrison of *Kurkara usu*. This is a small district of I'li. The town of the same name is now called King-shu ching. It ranks as a garrisoned town next to Kuldsha, and lies N.E. from it, on the river Kur, and on the road between Kuldsha and Urumtsi. See King-shu ching.

渠 搜 國 K'u-sau kwoh, the kingdom of Fahan, 500 *li* W. of the Blue Mountains. Ku-sau was the name of a mountain, and of a tribe of the Si-jung mentioned in the "Tribute of Yu."

古 滇 Ku-tien, an official name of the province of Yunnan. So Tien kwoh.

邛 Kung, the name of a tribe of I' on the S.W. of ancient China, now perpetuated in the name of a chau in Sech'uen.

公 方 Kung-fang, a title of the Shiogoon of Japan, sometimes applied to the Mikado. See T'ai kwan, and Tsiang Kiun.

宮 古 島 Kung-ku t'au, the largest of the Madjicosima group of Islands.

拱 宸 城 Kung-shin ching, in I'li, a garrisoned town near the river I'li, situated W. of Hwuiyuen ching, to which it is subordinate.

公 司 Kung Sz', the East India Company's factory at Canton. Traces of this name are still met with in all parts of China. The best cloth and the best opium are still called by their name.

恭 親 王 Kung-ts'in wang, a common name of Prince Kung. See Ho-shih-kung-wang. There are four orders of Princes in the Tartar court. 1st, 和 碩 親 王, *Ho-shih-ts'in-wang*, 2nd, 郡 王, *Kiun-wang*, 3rd, 貝 勒, *Pei-leh*, and 4th, 貝 子, *Pei-tsz'*. See Ho-shih-kung-t'sin-wang.

關 Kwan, the "Passes," or barriers, situated between Honan and Shensi, and in the latter province, and rendered famous in Chinese history as the "doors of the empire." See *Han-kuh kwan* and Kwan-chung.

關 閘 Kwan chah, the Barrier at Macao, built by the Chinese in 1573 to mark off the Portuguese territory.

關 中 Kwan-chung, the name of part of the present province of Shensi, in the Ts'in time, and of the ancient capital of the Western Han dynasty. There were four 關, at the four points of the compass, namely 東 有 函 谷 關, 南 有 嶢 關 武 關, 西 有 散 關, 北 有 蕭 關: See Kwan-si.

關 內 Kwan-lui, the name of Kwan-chung, as altered by the T'ang dynasty.

崑 崙 Kwan-lun, a range of mountains rendered famous in Chinese history and legend, separating Thibet from Chinese Turkestan and the desert of Gobi. It starts from the

Pushtikur knot, in Lat. 36° N. and runs along easterly, nearly parallel between that and the 35th degree. At the 92nd degree of Long. E., in the middle of its course, it divides into two ranges, one declining to the S.E., the Bayenkara, or the Snowy Mountains, and unites with the *Yun Ling*, or "Cloudy Mountains." The other branch bends northerly, and under the various names of Kilien Shan, In Shan and Ala shan, passes through Kansuh and Shensi to join the Inner Hing-ngan range. The Kwan-lun range is the Olympus of China, and the supposed source of its Fungshwui.

崐 嵛 層 斯 Kwan-lun-ts'ang-sz', a people in Thibet, incorrectly described by Rémusat as negroes. See Kwan-tun.

關 西 Kwan-si, the country to the W. of Shensi, answering to Lung-si, in Kansuh. *Kwan-si-tau* included part of Shensi province. See Kwan-chung and Kwan-tung.

裙 帶 路 K'wan-tai lu, "Petticoat-string path," the Chinese vulgar name for the city of Victoria, Hong-kong. See Hiang-kiang.

鯀 堤 Kwan-t'i, the name of a place in Chihli, where the beginning is said to have been made to drain off the waters of the deluge by *Kwan*, the father of the Great Yü. His labours have been much underrated. See *Pung-lai*.

崐 屯 Kwan-tun, the island of Pulo Condor. This is sometimes written Kwan-lun.

混 同 Kwan-t'ung, the "Mingled river," the name of the Sagalien river after its junction with the Songari. See Heh-lung kiang.

關 東 Kwan-tung, the country of Liautung, to the N. of China Proper, producing the best ginseng, named after it. There is a kind of ginseng produced in Kwan-si, a part of Shensi. Ginseng dealers use both Kwan-tung and Kwan-si on their signboards.

廣 州 府 Kwang-chau fu, the correct description of the provincial and departmental city of Canton. There is great probability in favour of this being the *Cattigara* of Ptolemy.

廣 仁 城 Kwang-jin ching, a garrisoned town lying N.W. of Hwuiyuen ching, near the Kirghis frontier.

廣 寧 城 Kwang-ning ching, a garrison subordinate to Shingking pun ching.

廣 寧 縣 Kwang-ning hien, a district in Kin-chau fu, in Lat. 41° 40′ N., and Long. 122° E. This town and that of I-chau are the first towns in Shingking, on entering, on the west the province, from Mongolia. The northern "guardian hill," the 醫 無 閭 山, I-wu-lu-shan, was situated in this district. See Wu chin.

鬼 方 Kwei-fang, or Kwei-fang kwoh, the country of the Hiung-nu, as named in the records of the Yin, or Shang dynasty. The opprobrious name Yang-kwei-tsz' is probably derived from this name applied to these Hunnish tribes.

歸 化 城 Kwei-hwa ching, a town on the borders of Shansi, the residence of a Tu-tung, or Adjutant-General over the tribe of Toumets.

桂 林 Kwei-lin, a name used in the time of Ts'in Chi-hwang for the region of Kwangsi. It is now applied to the premier fu and provincial capital of Kwangsi. This Kwei-lin fu, was once called 建 陵, Kien-ling.

歸 綏 城 Kwei-shu ching, or Kuku kotu, the "Blue city," a town in Shansi, the residence of a Ping-pei-tau, or officer connected with the control of the Toumets.

龜豆 Kwei-tau, a name for Manilla, as used by Chinese in the Straits. One of the Kypong islands, near the entrance of the Canton river is also known by this name.

龜茲國 Kwei-tsz' kwoh, Kuché, or Koutché, a district and town in Chinese Turkestan, formerly an independent state. See Ku-ché ching.

龜靜 Kwei-tsing, Cochin in South India. Ko-chih has been given as a name of this place in older writings.

國姓爺 Kwoh-sing-yé, the "Lord of the country's families," a name said by Von Siebold to be the original of Koxinga, or Kosenya, the piratical ruler of Formosa. See Ching chi-lung.

L

拉里城 La-li ching, H'lari, a town in the northern part of Anterior Thibet, bordering on Kokonor, with a district connected with it.

拉林城 La-lin ching, Larin ula, a garrison in the commandery of Petuné, in Kirin. It lies on the Songari river, between the town of Petuné and Altchucu, and has attracted some trade.

喇麻廟 Lah-ma-miáu, or Dolondo, in Lat. 42° 40′ N., and Long. 115° 20′ E., a large city and mart on the plains of Mongolia.

拉薩 La-sah, the capital of Thibet, is situated on the Dzangtsu river, about 12 leagues from its junction with the Yaru-tsangbu, in Lat. 29° 30′ N., and Long. 91° 40′ E. It is the largest town in this part of Asia, and is famous as the headquarters of the lamas. See Pu-tah-la.

拉達克 La-tah-keh, Ladak, or Leh, sometimes called Mar-yul, a wool-producing country, bounded N. by the "Onion mountains," E. by Rodok and Gardok, S. and S.W. by the Himalayas, separating it from Cashmere, and N.W. by Beltistan, or little Thibet. The Indus flows through this independent country, which has preserved its separate existence by the peaceful and propitiatory temper of its princes, who send annual presents to adjoining rulers, as a kind of friendly acknowledgment of the benefits of the caravan trade passing through this territory. Leh, the capital, is in Lat. 44° 10′ N., and Long. 77° 45′ E.

萊子國 Lai-tsz' kwoh, a district near the Shantung promontory, now called Teng-chau fu. This Teng-chau, is to be distinguished from Tung-chau in Chihli, on the line of the caravan route from Kalgan, by Dunba to Tientsin, prescribed in the Russo-Chinese treaty.

覽房 Lan-fang, Lampong in Sumatra.

藍帽回子 Lan-mau-hwui-tsz', the "blue-cap-hwui tsz'," a name applied to the Jews, who came to China in greatest number from Persia. From this country, in part, came the first Mahommedans, who were Turks, or Kisilbash, wearing the red fez-cap.

蘭摩 Lan-mo, Rama in India.

琅琊 Lang-ya, or 狼牙修, Lang-ya-siu, the island or islands of Linga, or Lingon between Borneo and Sumatra. See Mencius, Book I. part II. chap. IV. Legge's ed: This was the name of one of Ts'in Chi-hwang's forty prefectures or principalities. See Jau kwoh.

老撾 Lau-chwa, the Laos tribes who live between Yunnan, Annam, and Siam.

樓蘭 Lau-lan, the name given to Shen-shen, before the Han dynasty.

筹子 Lau-tsz', the Laos and Shan tribes tributary to the adjacent states of Burmah, Siam and Annam. They are sometimes called K'ih-lau. See Ye-lang.

老萬山 Lau-wan-shan, the largest of the Ladrone Islands.

犂軒 Li-han, or Li-chien, the name of a country known to the Chinese in the Han period, and placed by them to the W. of the "Western Sea." It may have been the Latin, or Roman empire. See Ta-t'sin.

理藩院 Li-fan-yuen, the Colonial or Foreign office in Peking. See T'sung-li-ya-men.

里馬 Li-ma, or Bima, the Malay kingdom in the E. part of the island of Sumbawa. It formerly sent much sandal-wood and sapan-wood to China.

利瑪竇 Li-ma-tuh, the Chinese name of Matteo Ricci, who was in China from 1582 to 1610.

里猫柔 Li-mau-jau, the Dyaks of Borneo.

孅戎 Li-jung, a frontier state in the N. of China, in the time of the Tsin dynasty.

裏塘 Li-t'ang, or Lithang, a town of some importance in Thibet.

黎峒 Li-t'ung, the Taic aborigines of Hainan and the adjacent mainland.

利未亞 Li-wei-ya, Libya, or Africa.

梁州 Liang chau, a name of K'ai-fung fu in Honan, during the Tung Wei rule. This is also the name of one of Yü's provinces, including Sech'uen, with parts of Kansuh, Shensi, Hupeh, and perhaps of Kweichau.

梁公府 Liang-kung-fu, the British Legation in Peking, formerly the palace of the Duke Liang, as the name implies.

遼河 Liau ho, the river which drains the large area of the eastern half of the province of Shingking, and runs into the gulf of the same name. It is said to be not now navigable for large vessels much beyond Newchwang. As one of the "six streams," it was anciently called 遼水.

遼西 Liau-si, an old name of the time of Ts'in Chi-hwang, applied to what is now Kin-chau fu in Shingking, and Chang-li hien in Pehchihli.

獠子 Liau-tsz', the Laos tribes. See Lau-tsz'.

遼東 Liau-tung, or Shingking, one of Ts'in Chi-hwang's prefectures, named after the Liau river. It comprised, before the Manchu conquest, only that part near the gulf, and a part of the present Pehchihli.

遼陽州 Liau-yang chau, in Shingking, a district of Fung-t'ien fu, in Lat. 41° 10′ N., and Long. 123° 27′ E. Liau-yang was the name of one of the 12 provinces of China, under the Yuen dynasty.

遼陽城 Liau-yang ching, in Shingking, subordinate to the head garrison.

琳 國 Lin kwoh, a country in Central Asia, 9,000 *li* from Singan fu, yielding excellent pears.

臨 安 Lin-ngau, a name of Hangchow in Chekiang, an old capital of China. To this place of rest came Kau-tsung of the Nan Sung dynasty, in A.D. 1129, and many of the same line made it their residence. See King-sz'.

林 邑, Lin-yih, a place said to be identical with Jeh-nan and Chen-ching, from which much gold and silver were formerly brought to China. Hwan-yang is said to be another name of this Cambodian kingdom. In some Chinese maps Lin-yih is placed to the W. of Chen-ching.

嶺 南 Ling-nan, the country S. of the Meiling, or as they are sometimes called, the Great Stack mountains, forming one of the 15 *tau* of the T'ang dynasty, and answering to the Kwang-nan of the Sung dynasty. This was divided into two *lu*, Kwang-nan-si and Kwang-nan-tung, the origin of the present provinces of Kwang-si and Kwang-tung.

伶 仃 Ling-ting, the island of Lintin, or the "Orphan," lying to the W.N.W. of Urmston Bay.

琉 球 國 Liu-kiu kwoh, the tributary state of Luchu, or Lewchew ("Pendent globes"). These islands formerly composed three petty kingdoms, called Chung Shan (中 山), Shan-nan, (山 南), and Shan-peh, (山 北), whose chiefs sent tribute to Hung-wu of the Ming. Chu K'wan, an officer of the Sui emperor Ta Nieh, visited the country. Some confusion exists between this country and Borneo, in Chinese books. See Shau-ni.

流 沙 Liu-sha, the desert of Gobi. See Sha-moh.

羅 刹 國 Lo-chah kwoh, a country of red-headed black savages, between Lin-yih and Siam. It was visited by the Chinese embassy from the Sui emperor, Ta Nieh, to the king of Siam.

倮 國 Lo kwoh, a country of unclad savages in the W., fearless of wild beasts.

維 布 淖 爾 Lo-pu-nau-rh, the modern name of Lake Lop Nor. This lake lies on the edge of a desert, in an uninhabited region. Into it, in Long. 38° E., after a course of some 1,400 miles, there runs the largest inland river in the world, the Tarim. See Pu-chang hai.

邏 娑 Lo-so, the name of a city in Turfan.

羅 多 克 城 Lo-to-keh ching, the town of Rodok in Nari, on the borders of Thibet, a little to the S.E. of Ladak. Under the Ming dynasty it was a small independent state. To the E. of this town, with its fort surrounded by four monasteries and 150 houses, commences the Aksaichin, or "White desert of China," which runs parallel to the great desert of Gobi.

樂 浪 Loh-lang, a tributary state of the Han dynasty, in all probability the same as Corea or Sin-lo. See next.

樂 浪 海 Loh-lang hai, the sea between the coast of Chekiang and the islands of Japan, in which Chinese geographers place Japan. This name was also applied to the Yellow Sea, after the name of Corea.

洛 陽 Loh-yang, the capital of China under the Eastern Han, A.D. 25. It is now a district town in Honan fu in the province of Honan. See I-kien. It is asserted by Biot, that the old city was somewhat to the W. of the present district town. See Lung-shau-shan.

瀘 江 Lú kiang, a name of the Yangtsz' Kiang, in its upper part, so called from one of its tributaries in Sech'uen. See Kin-sha kiang.

鷺 江 Lu kiang, or 鷺 門, Lu-men, or 鷺 島 Lu-tau, are names used in Chinese poetical compositions for the island of Amoy, and its port. These names are derived from that of the 鷺 鷥, Lu-sz', or White Egret (Herodias euophotes), which annually frequents the islands of Amoy, Quemoy and the large number of islets of the bay. This bird with perhaps other species, is used in the decorations of civil officers, the 白 鷺 peh lu being the distinctive badge of the sixth civil rank. The flesh of this bird is recommended in the Pen T'sau as very nourishing. This Lu-kiang is to be carefully distinguished from the next, which see.

潞 江 Lu kiang, the Irawaddy river (Pauthier). See Nu kiang. Amoy is sometimes spoken of as Lu-kiang, from the number of egrets to be seen on the island.

魯 西 亞 Lu-si-ya, the Japanese term for Russia. See Ngo-lo-si.

呂 宋 Lu-sung, Lucon or Luconia, the Philippine Islands. See Siau-lu-sung.

六 詔 Lu-cháu, the country in the present province of Yunnan, called Caraian by Marco Polo. This name strictly applies to the six leaders of these mountain tribes, supposed to be Karens or Wu-man. See Yueh-sih-chau.

坴 賴 Luh-lai, the Laos tribes of the dry and woody regions of the S. The first character is perhaps a mistake for 陸, Luh. The Lo-lo tribes in Yunnan spoken of by Duhalde, may perhaps be indicated by these characters. See also Sien-lo.

內 Lui. For words commencing with this character, see Nui, the more correct word.

龍 賴 Lung-lai, a name of the Laos tribes.

龍 首 山 Lung-shau shan, the situation of the capital city, or imperial residence of the sovereigns of the Sui dynasty who first resided at Chang-ngan, or Singan fu (Shensi). This site was 33 li to the N. of the city proper of Chang-ngan. Much uncertainty exists as to the precise situations of many of the ancient capitals and other cities, which by no means necessarily coincided exactly with the sites bearing the same name in successive dynasties, or at the present time. Thus for instance 建 業, Kien-yeh is referred by some Chinese authors to 上 元 縣, Shang-yuen hien, and not to 江 甯 府 Kiang-ning fu, the present dynastic name of Nanking, See Lohyang.

隴 西 Lung-si, a prefecture of the Ts'in dynasty answering to a part of Kansuh. This is probably identical with the Kwan-si of a later period. There is a Lung-si hien in Kansuh at the present time.

隴 束 Lung-tung, an old name of P'ing-liang fu in Kansuh.

巒 江 Lwan-kiang, an old name of I'-ching hien, in Yang-chau fu (Kiangsu). See Chinch'uen.

M

馬 湖 江 Ma-hu kiang, a name of the Kin-sha kiang or Ta kiang.

麻 六 呷 Ma-luh-kiah, Malacca. See Man-lah-kia.

馬八兒 Ma-pah-rh, M'abar, or Malabar, on the eastern side of Cape Comorin. Pauthier identifies the characters *Muh-lu-pa* with M'abar.

瑪珀穆達賴 Ma-peh-moh-tah-lai, a lake in Thibet, forming with another sacred lake, Langga Nor, the head-waters of the Indus.

馬辰 Ma-shin, Banjermassin, a port in the S. of Borneo, formerly the capital of a kingdom. This is identified by some with that part of Borneo sometimes called *P'o-lo*.

馬蹟 Ma-tsih, Gutzlaff Island, off the mouth of the Yangtsz'.

抹羅短吡國 Mah-lo-tan-chih kwoh, a country in South India, said to yield Baroos camphor.

買賣鎭 Mai-mai chin, the name "Trading-mart" incorrectly applied to Kiachta, Urga, Kalgan and other similar towns on the frontier. *Mai-mai-chin* is really a small hamlet, and the trade is carried on near it, and not in Kiachta. The same name is applied to the Chinese town, distant four miles from Urga. Kiachta is situated on a creek running into the Selenga in Lat. 50° 21' N., and Long. 106° 28' E. Its importance as a place of Russo-Chinese trade is decreasing rapidly.

蠻 Man, the southern aborigines of China, the *Manji* of Marco Polo. They were divided into eight tribes, and reached as far north as the Yangtsz'.

蠻子 Man-tsz', wild aborigines of Sech'uen, living in caves. They gave their name to other tribes.

滿喇加 Man-lah-kia, Malacca, or some Malaysian kingdom, to the S. of Tsiampa. Its king *Silahpaher Suhtah* sent tribute to China in the third year of the reign of Yung-loh of the Ming dynasty. It was formerly a tributary of the kingdom of Siam. Stream-tin is mentioned in the Pen T'sau as coming to China from this place.

茫咖薩 Mang-kia-sah, Macassar, a city and district in the S. of the island of Celebes, now belonging to the Dutch, and called by them Vlaardingen.

毛明安 Mau-ming-ngan, or Mao Mingan, a small tribe of Mongols, living S. of the Great Desert, 800 *li* N.W. of Kalgan.

默克國 Meh-keh kwoh, Mecca, or Arabia itself. See T'ien-fang kwoh.

墨爾根城 Meh-rh-kan ching, Merguen, a garrisoned town of some trade, in Tsitsihar, situated on the Nonni river, about 40 leagues above the capital of the province. It is the residence of a commandant ruling over all the tracts lying between the E. bank of the Nonni and the Inner Hing-ngan range. It is in Lat. 46° 10' N., and Long. 124° 40' E.

默德那 Meh-teh-na, city of Medina, or Yathreb, 300 miles to the N. of Mecca.

湄江 Mei kiang, the Meikong, or Mekong, or Cambodia river. This river, in its upper waters in Yunnan, is only a dangerous torrent. See Nan-chang kiang and Ho-ti kiang.

美國 Mei kwoh, the United States of America. See Hwa-k'i kwoh.

美洛居 Mei-loh-ku, the Molucca Islands.

彌勒佛 Mi-leh-fuh, the Buddha of the future calpa, called Maitreya in Sanscrit. Kwanyin and Ju-lai-fuh are the deities of the present calpa. See Ju-lai-fuh.

米六合 Mi-luh-hoh. See Meilohku.

彌斯爾 Mi-sz'-rh, Egypt, or Mitzraim. It is somtimes written Mi-sz' kwoh

廟 島 Miau t'au, a group of islands near Tungchow (Shantung), marking the ancient coast line.

苗 子 Miau-tsz', the aboriginal inhabitants of certain mountainous districts, and possibly of other parts of China. They consist of more than eighty tribes, scattered over the provinces of Kweichau, Hunan, Kwangtung, Kwangsi, and Yunnan, with doubtful branches in Chekiang, Hupeh and other provinces. Their dialect is mainly Taic, marking their affinity with the Laos tribes of Burmah, Siam, and Annam, and the Karens, or Wu-man. They are to be distinguished from the Man-tsz', of which there are tribes in Kwei-ting hien and Tu-yun fu (Kweichau) for instance. They are Buddhist in their religious practices. They have never been subdued by the Imperial armies, but give rise to occasional hostilities of a local character, as between themselves, or against their natural enemies and cowardly oppressors, the Chinese officers.

儌 偐 Mieh-ts'ien, a Tungusic tribe on the N.E. related to the Manchus, and notoriously deceitful.

沔 水 Mien-shwui, a name of the Han river before the period of the San-kwoh-chí. See Yang-shwui. Hankow was once Mien-k'au.

緬 甸 Mien-tien, or Mien kwoh, the kingdom of Ava or Burmah. See A-wa.

肦 頓 國 Mih-kieh kwoh, the country of the Massagetæ, or Indo-Scythians. See Yueh-ti.

密 國 Mih kwoh, or 密 須 國, Mih-su kwoh, the name of Ling-tai hien (Kansuh) during the Chau period. It was changed to the present style by the Sui dynasty.

閩 Min, the official designation of the province of Fukien. See Min-chung.

閩 中 Min chung, the name of one of the principalities or prefectures of the Ts'in dynasty included in Peh-yueh, and forming part of the Yang-chau of Yü's time. As only a part of Canton province was included, with Fukien, under this name, the term is properly applied at the present time to Fukien. There is a Min-ts'ing hien in Fukien (Fuhchau fu).

明 州 府 Ming-chau fu, the name of Ning-po fu during the T'ang dynasty. The Sung and the Yuen called it 慶 元, King-yuen. The Ming sovereigns restored the old name of Ming-chau fu, but afterwards changed it for the present style of 寧 波 府, or 審 波 府, having adopted the name of 明, Ming for their dynasty. It is to be observed that in wise policy, the present dynasty has adhered to the same idea of "clear," in simply exchanging T'sing for Ming.

岷 江 Min kiang, a name of the Yangtsz' in its upper course, arising from a confusion as to the main stream.

明 都 Ming-tu, Tonquin, or Tungking, the "eastern capital" of Cochin China. Tung-ming, a name somewhat resembling these, is the old designation of what is now Lan-í hien (Honan).

摩 伽 陁 國 Mo-kia-to kwoh, the country of Magadha. See P'o-so kwoh, and the next.

摩 竭 提 國 Mo-kieh-t'i kwoh, the country of Magadha, the birthplace of Buddha, answering to the modern district of Behar. The popular dialect of this place, became the Pali or Fan, the sacred or classical language of the Buddhists of Ceylon. Pali is called Magadabasa by the Burmese.

摩尼 Mo-ni, the name of the place where Buddha is said to have resided with the assembled gods.

母撒 Mo-sah, or Mu-sa, the name for Moses, used by the Chinese Mahommedans. Mo-si is the term used in Christian publications in Chinese.

摩土羅 Mo-t'u-lo, Madura, in the Carnatic.

謨罕驀德 Moh-han-meh-teh, Mohammed, the "renowned" as the Arabic means. The character 穆, Moh, sometimes used by itself for Mohammed, comes nearer to this idea.

靺鞨 Moh-hoh, a name of the Nu-chin, or Nu-chih tribe, famous for their rubies and other gems. They were divided into seven tribes. See Wuh-kih.

穆胡 Moh-hu, the Mahommedans. See Moh-han-meh-teh.

穆迦 Moh-kia, a name for Mecca, much used in the Straits. See T'ien-fang kwoh.

秣陵 Moh-ling, the name of Nanking during Ts'in Chi-hwang's reign.

穆民 Moh-min, the Mahommedan people. See Hwui-hwui.

魔泥 Moh-ni, or Mo-ni, (摩尼), the Manichæan sect, descended from the Mani of Persia. They once had places of worship and adherents in China.

莫傜 Moh-yau, the inhabitants of a Liberia, spoken of in Chinese legends, whose ancestors had "never served" any lord. Their character is well maintained by their descendants, the Hunan men of Chang-sha fu.

慕容氏 Mu-yung-shi, a branch of the Sien-pi, the ancestors of the Liau.

木邦 Muh-pang, a division of the country of Peh-tsi.

木頭城 Muh-t'u ching, the wooden palisade in Shingking.

蒙番 Mung-fan, a foreign tribe to the W. of Sech'uen.

蒙古 Mung-ku, Mongolia, or the Mongolians. This vast country is inhabited by the nomadic Mongols, and is divided into 內蒙古, Nui Mung-ku, and 外蒙古, Wai Mung-ku, or Inner and Outer Mongolia. 泰赤烏, T'ai ch'ih-wu, and the 克列, K'eh-lieh, with the 塔塔兒, Tah-tah-rh, were Mongol names.

蒙古人 Mung-ku jin, the Mongols, who received their name of Kukai Mongöl, from Genghis Khan, to distinguish his own tribe as the "Celestial people," from the Tatars, "tributaries." There is no proof that the Chinese call themselves "Celestials," as most persons assume.

滿洲 Mwan cháu, the country of Manchuria.

滿人 Mwan jin, the Manchus, or Mandshus, a Tungusic race, which with the Lamutes of Siberia form the Eastern branch. They now rule the Mongolic and Chinese peoples, formerly their "celestial" superiors.

滿軍 Mwan-kiun, the Tartar bannermen. See Pah k'i.

滿喇 Mwan-lah, the Mullah, a Mahommedan name used for the Jewish Rabbi at K'ai-fung fu. The Jewish remnant seems to have become merged into the kindred faith of the followers of Islam. See K'ai-fung fu, Ts'ing-chin kiau and Yih-tsz'-loh-nieh-tien.

N

奈 曼　Nai-man, a tribe of Mongols, 600 *li* N.W. of the Hifung gate.

南 裳　Nan-chang, or 南 掌, Nan-chang, the capital of the tribes of the South Laos. The Laos, belonging to the Taïc class of the Turanian family, are called *Shyan*, or *Layn-sayn* by the Burmese, and *Lanian*, or *Laniangh* by European writers of the 17th century.

南 掌 江　Nan-chang kiang, the Meikong river, giving its name to the South Laos tribes.

南 州　Nan cháu, the Southern provinces of China. See Nan-yueh.

南 詔　Nan-cháu, the style of the chiefs of Laos tribes bordering on Yunnan. This term is sometimes applied to their country, the Caraïan of Marco Polo.

南 城　Nan-ching, a name of Nan-chang fu city (Kiangsi), also called Hung-tu.

南 海　Nan-hai, the Indian Ocean. The gulf of Tonquin, or any part of the sea off the coast of the S. of China may be understood by this term, according to the context. One of Ts'in Chi-hwang's provinces in the present Kwangtung was known by this name, still perpetuated in the Nan-hai hien.

南 海 觀 世 音　Nan-hai Kwan-shi-yin, Kwanyin, the Goddess of Mercy.

南 畿　Nan kí, Kiangnan or Nanking. See Kiang-ning.

南 交　Nan-kiau, a name first given to a country S. of Cochin China, but commonly interchanged with the next.

南 交 阯 地　Nan-kiau-chí-ti, a name of Cochin China. See Yueh-nan.

南 京　Nan-king, one of the ancient capitals of China, of which since the days of the "First Emperor," there have been at least eighteen changes amongst nine principal places of imperial residence. See Kiang-ning and Kin-ling. The Kin Tartars called Ka'i-fung fu by this name. Nanking was also known to the Ming sovereigns by the name of Ying-t'ien.

南 蠻 國　Nan-man kwoh, a name of Cambodia. See Chin-lah. Nan-man is another name of Ku-luh hien, in Shun-teh fu (Pehchihli).

南 山　Nan shan, the Kwanlun mountains. See T'ien shan.

南 灣　Nan wan, the Praya Grande at Macao.

南 無 阿 彌 陀 佛　Nan-wu A-mi-to-fuh, an invocation to Amita Buddha, "Honour to the boundless Buddha."

南 越　Nan-yueh, an old name of Canton province, sometimes applied to Annam or Tonquin. See Yueh-nan.

那 霸　Na-pa, the port of the capital of the Liukiu islands. See Shau-ni.

愛 琿 城　Ngai-hwan ching, Aaihom or Aykhom, a town on the Amur, opposite Sagalien ula, built in the Ming period to repress the incursions of the Mongols. It is now in ruins.

哀 牢 夷　Ngai-lau-í, a tribe of the Laos, connected with the Karens, and said to be skilful in dyeing and embroidering cloth. See Nan chau.

安 阜 城　Ngan-fau ching, a garrison near Kurkara usu.

安 南 國　Ngan-nan kwoh, the kingdom of Annam, or Cochin China. Much trade was carried on with China before the recent Yunnan troubles. See Yueh-nan. There is a kind of cinnamon, called *Ngan pien kwei*, brought from Annam, in very high repute.

安石國 Ngan-shih kwoh, Cabul. Persimmons were brought from this country during the Han dynasty.

安西 Ngan-si, a name of Si-ngan fu under the Yuen dynasty.

安息 Ngan-sih, or 安西, Ngan-si, the country of the Parthians. The drug benzoin is named after this country, from which it was first brought.

安汶 Ngan-wan, the island of Amboyna, near Ceram, one of the Moluccas.

安邑 Ngan-yih, the capital of the Hia dynasty, answering to the present Hia hien, in P'ing-yang fu (Shansi).

敖漢 Ngau-han, a tribe of Mongols, living beyond the Hifung gate of the Great Wall.

歐羅巴 Ngau-lo-pa, the continent of Europe. See Ta-si-yang.

澳門 Ngau-men, Macao, situated in the district of Hiang-shan. See A-ma-ngau.

額魯特 Ngeh-lu-teh, the Eleuths, or Songares, a Mongolian tribe formerly exercising independent sovereignty over the *T'ien Shan Peh Lu*, Khoten, and even more extensive territory, after the expulsion of the Mongols from China. They are now scattered all over I'li.

俄國 Ngo kwoh, the Russian empire. The Russians themselves speak of the Chinese as the Kitai. See K'i-tan.

俄羅斯 Ngo-lo-si, the usual translation of the word Russia into Chinese. This is perhaps a transference of the Mongol word *Oaroos*, or *Oros* into Chinese, that being the name for Russia, first known to the Chinese during the early part of the Ming dynasty. The intervention of the *Kara Kitai*, exterminated by the Mongols, after a long rule over the north of China, had prevented any knowledge of China Proper. The Chinese are however still called *Kitai*, by the Russians, after this northern race.

俄國牛綠 Ngo kwoh niu-luh, the defeated Russians, called Albasins, who were brought to Peking after the attack on the fort of Albasin, or Yacsa, in 1684. They were formed into a kind of troop, and provision for their spiritual wants was the cause of the establishment of the Russian ecclesiastical mission at Peking. See Ya-keh-sah. They are now nearly extinct as a foreign people.

鄂渚 Ngoh-chü, an ancient name for Wuchang and Hanyang. Wuchang was the capital of the Wu dynasty, for a time.

鄂羅斯 Ngoh-lo si, Russia, as written in Chinese official works.

鄂爾多斯 Ngoh-rh-to-sz', the Ortous tribe of Mongols, on the N. borders of Shansi, W. of Kweihwa ching, and E. of the Kalkas. They are arranged under seven banners, and their territory is nearly surrounded by the Yellow River. This as well as other of the Mongolian tribes, rendered valuable assistance to the Manchu invaders of China, and they are therefore peculiarly favoured by the ruling dynasty.

鄂登 Ngoh-tang, Oden, a city of Tartary.

鄂敦他拉 Ngoh-tun-ta-la, Hotun tala, the Mongolian name for *Sing-suh-hai*, or "Sea of Constellations," the network of streams and pools at the source of the Yellow River. See Sing-suh-hai.

尼婆羅 Ni-p'o-lo, Nepaul. See Koh-rh-keh.

尼 布 楚 Ni-pú-tsú, Nipchu, a town in the Tuchetu Khanate of the Kalkas, on the Russian frontier. It is in Lat 51° 49′ N., and is the place where, after much delay, the Chinese and Russians signed a treaty in 1689.

呢 是 Ni-shi, Pulo Nias, W. of Sumatra.

俚 子 Ni-tsz', the wild tribes of Annam. See To-lo-men.

鄴 郡 Nieh-kiun, an old name of a part of the present Chang-teh fu (Honan). It was the seat of the capital of Peh-tsí, one of the many states of the Wu Tai, still called by this name in documents.

聶 拉 本 城 Nieh-la-pun ching, Nielam, or Ngialam, a town and district on the ·S, frontiers of Ulterior Thibet.

寧 海 縣 Ning-hai hien, a district of Fung-t'ien fu, in Shingking.

寧 夏 Ning-hia, or Egrigaia, a town in Kansuh, visited by Marco Polo, and then containing many Nestorian Christians in its prefecture. The researches of Panthier tend to show that Egrigaia was the name of the kingdom, of which Ninghia, identified with Calatia, was the capital. See Wuh-lah-hai.

寧 古 塔 城 Ning-ku-tah ching, Ningkuta, or Ningunta, the largest town in the province of Kirin, the residence of the officers commanding the south-eastern part of Kirin, lying on the Sea of Japan. It lies on the Hurha, a branch of the Songari river, in Lat. 44° 55′ N., and Long. 128° E.

寧 波 府 Ning-po fu, the city of Ningpo, the *Liam-po* of the Portuguese, where the first development, on a large scale, of European intercourse with China took place. See Sz'-ming. Ming-chau fu.

牛 莊 Niu-chwang, the inland town mentioned in the Treaty of 1858, but which from the river being silted up, was unfit for foreign trade, and was exchanged for Ying-tsz', which is still called Niuchwang. See Yingtsz' and Yun-tsz'.

·牛 莊 城 Niu-chwang ching, a garrison subordinate to the head garrison of Shingking, in Lat. 41° 20′ 25″ N., and Long. 122° 41′ 50″ E. situated some 80 miles up the river Liáu, or 80 miles by road, from Yingtsz', the treaty-port.

牛 頭 山 Niu-t'u shan, a mountain near Khoten whence jade used to come in large quantities. It is curious that carved portions of this mineral, sometimes called nephrite, or axe-stone, have been met with in Europe under circumstances which may point to these jade articles having been brought from the far east. Chinese seals of some such material have also been apparently found in Ireland.

女 直 Nu-chih, } Tungusic tribes, ancestors of the Kin, and progenitors of the present Manchu
女 真 Nu-chin, } reigning family. See Suh-shin-shí. Wuh-kih.

奴 夷 Nu-í, a name applied to the Laos tribes inhabiting parts of Yunnan, as well as to certain Turkic tribes on the borders of Nepaul.

怒 江 Nu kiang, the old name of the Irawaddy river. The Mongols made this one of the Sz' tuh of China. See Ya-lu-tsang-pu, and Lu-kiang.

女 子 國 Nu-tsz' kwoh, one of the many countries of Amazons, mentioned in Chinese writings, to the N. of Wu-hien. There was a Nu-kwoh 1,000 *li* to the E. of Fu-sang.

內 番 Nui-fan, the tributary "foreign" tribes in Sech'uen and Formosa, or any province within China Proper.

內 海 Nui-hai, the Caspian Sea. This is sometimes written Ni-hai.

內 夷 Nui-í, the wild aborigines or mountain tribes of Kweichau, &c.

內 史 Nui-shi, one of Ts'in Chi-hwang's forty prefectures, including part of Shensi.

內 土 Nui-tu, China, the "Inner Land." This is often written 內 地, Nui-ti.

儂 人 Nung-jin, an aboriginal tribe in Yunnan. This name is used in some dialects for villagers, but in the Amoy dialect it is an offensive term.

O

阿 城 O-ching. See A-ching.

阿 房 宮 O-fang-kung, the harem of Ts'in Chi-hwang at Si-ngan fu. See A-ching.

阿 哥 O-ko. See Tai-tsz'.

閼 氏 Oh-shi, the style of the consort of the Turkic sovereign, himself called 匈 奴, Hiung-nu, the name usually given to this tribe. This Oh-shi is directed to be pronounced as 焉 支, Yen-chí. See Tan-u and Hiu-chü.

阿 丹 O-tan. See A-tan. This name for Adam seems preferable to the one used by the delegates of the Missionary Societies, namely 亞 當, Ya-tang. The latter is however founded on a tradition given in the 龍 文 鞭 影, a book of the Ming dynasty, giving an account of ancient personages. The account is said to be derived from the 西 經, Si King, or "Western Classic," a very good name for the Bible.

P

巴 Pa, the name of an ancient principality in the S.E. of Sech'uen, of which we have a trace in the Pa Hi, or jugglery of the streets. See also Koh-lah-pa.

巴 林 Pa-lin, or Barin, a tribe of Mongols, living 720 li N.E. of Kaupeh k'au, and W. of Kirin.

巴 爾 庫 爾 Pa-rh-ku-rh, Barkul, called by the Chinese Chinsi fu, and now attached to Kansuh. It lies at the E. spur of the T'ien shan, near the lake Barkul. The garrisoned town is also called I'ho hien. See Chinsi fu.

把 實 Pa-shih, Passir, on the S.E. of Borneo, formerly an independent kingdom, yielding much gold dust. See Wan-lai.

巴蜀 Pa-shuh, the western of the three states into which China was divided A.D. 221, at the end of the Eastern Han dynasty. It is now used as the official designation of the province of Sech'uen. See Pa.

巴達克山 Pa-tah-keh-shan, a long mountain valley, situated between the Belur Tagh and the Ridge of Pamere. It belongs to Bokhara, and is celebrated for its unrivalled rubies, its iron, sulphur, salt and lapis lazuli. It is well watered by the Oxus. The chief town, Fyzabad, is in Lat. 37° N., and Long. 70° 35' E.

巴且 Pa-tan, an ancient seaport near Kü-lan, or Quilon, frequented by Chinese merchants.

巴塘 Pa-t'ang, Bathang, called by Huc "the plain of Cows," a rich valley in Thibet, with a town of the same name, containing a Chinese garrison.

巴圖魯 Pa-t'u-lu, a Manchu order of knighthood, or peerage. A lordship or gratuity formerly accompanied the distinction, which is augmented by various qualifying titles in Manchu or Chinese. The word itself is equivalent to the characters *ying hiung*, a hero. See Tieh-mau-tsz'-wang.

把東 Pa-tung, Padang, on the W. coast of Sumatra. It formerly yielded much Baros camphor.

巴顏喀喇 Pa-yen-k'eh-lah, Bayenkara, a high range of mountains, commencing W. of the T'sing-hai. It is sometimes called Siueh-ling.

八旗 Pah-k'i, the "eight banners," under which the Manchus are marshalled. They have a nominal strength of 80,000 men to each banner, or altogether 640,000 men. Each banner is distinguished by its colour. Four banners are wholly yellow, white, red and blue, and four have these colours bordered.

八百媳婦國 Pah-peh-sih-fuh kwoh, the *Cangigu* of Marco Polo, inhabited by the North Laos tribes having their capital at Chiangmai. See Chau-mei.

八宛 Pah-yuen, the "Eight Pasturages," a place in Inner Mongolia, near the ancient Mongol capital, K'aiping.

拜城 Pai ching, Bai, a town in Ili, about 25 miles W. of Sairam. This was formerly known as *Pa-lu-kia*.

拜弟城 Pai-ti ching, a town placed in Chinese maps, in Anterior Thibet

彭城 P'ang ching, the capital of a small kingdom belonging to *Tsü-pa-wang*, the enemy of Kau-tsü, the founder of the Han dynasty. It is now the department of 徐州府, Su-chau fu in Kiangsu. The name dates from the Ts'in.

彭亨 P'ang-hiang, Paghan, or Pegassim, the ancient capital of Burmah.

澎湖 P'ang-hu, the Pescadore islands, twenty-one of which are inhabited. They form a *ting* division, attached to Formosa. The Dutch seized Fischer's island in 1624.

榜葛剌 Pang-koh-lah, the country of Bengal. See Tan kwoh.

彭蠡 P'ang-li, a former name of the Poyang Lake.

庖犧 P'au Hi, a name of Fuh Hi or Fohi.

暴暴 Pau-pau, Papua, or the island of New Guinea. China was probably supplied during the Ming period, with slaves called *Kwan-lun-nu* from Papua. This is sometimes called *Pa-pu-ya*, as in the *Yih-t'ung-yü-t'u*.

白 霫 Peh-chih, a large country in the N., cold and marshy, and divided into three provinces. See Hi-chih.

北 直 隸 Peh-chih-li, or Chih-li, a name formerly given to the metropolitan province (now called in short Chih-li), to distinguish it from Kiangnan, or Nan-chih-li, the old location of the seat of government, where many of the boards, or departments, of control lingered for a long time after the change of capital.

北 海 Peh-hai, a name given by the Chinese to the Gulf of Pehchihli, but usually assigned in foreign works to Lake Baikal in Irkutsk. Here, on its southern side, was the original seat of the Uigurs, according to Persian writers.

北 蝦 夷 Peh-hia-í, the island of Tarakai, or Northern Yesso, opposite the mouth of the Sagalien river. It is called, incorrectly, Sagalien in European maps. The Japanese call it Kr'afto. On some Chinese maps this island is apparently named Ku-yeh-t'au. A large Russian garrison is now permanently established on the southern coast of this island, and it will be of considerable importance as a military and telegraphic station.

北 京 Peh-king, Peking, the capital of China, called *Khan baligh*, or *Khanpalik*, by the Mongols. This name was corrupted into *Khambalu* by the Chinese, and *Cambaluc* by Marco Polo. The "Paquin of Sinæan kings," of Milton, or the Paguin of Lord Bacon, it was considered to be a seaport by the latter. It is in Lat. 39° 54′ 13″ N., and Long. 116° 27′ E. It has been the capital since 1411. The city having nine gates, is also called 九 門 城 Kiu men ching, and the Manchu governor was formerly styled after this name.

白 鴿 巢 Peh-koh ch'au, the "Dove's nest," the garden at Macao in which the grotto of Camoens is situated.

白 蘭 Peh-lan, a tribe of the Kiang, living near Tangut, remarkable for their military prowess.

白 民 國 Peh-min kwoh, a country of Albinoes, mentioned in the *Shan-hai-king*. See Yang-peh-t'u.

北 峩 Peh-ngo, Pegu, formerly a part of the Burman empire.

北 平 Peh-p'ing, the present city of Tsun-chau fu in Pehchihli, a temporary capital of Yung-loh. See Lung-shan-shan.

白 山 Peh-shan, a snow-capped peak in the T'ien Shan range, which was an active volcano as late as the middle of the 7th century.

白 塔 Peh-t'ah, the "white tower" on the Yellow River.

北 地 郡 Peh-ti kiun, an old principality, including at least Kansuh with other regions in Shensi.

北 亭 Peh-ting, the country of Bichbalish about Lake Tengez, or Balkash, beyond Tarbagatai.

北 庭 山 Peh-ting shan, a volcanic mountain in Turfan, yielding sal ammoniac from fissures in its sides. This drug is in much repute as an expensive ophthalmic remedy.

百 濟 Peh-tsí, or Hakusai, a kingdom in the south-eastern part of Corea, afterwards united with Sin-lo, from whence in the year 284 B.C. the Japanese obtained Chinese books, and a knowledge of Chinese characters. Compare another account under Wang-jin. The second best quality of ginseng was formerly brought from here. One of the Wu Tai states had this name.

白頭人 Peh-t'u-jin, a name used in Canton for Moors and Parsees. See Yang-peh-t'u.

伯都納城 Peh-t'u-nah ching, the garrison of Petuné ula, a ting department, called Peh-tu-nah li-sz'-ting, in the north-western part of Kirin. It is a place of considerable trade, being accessible from all quarters by means of the Songari and Amur rivers, and their numerous branches. It is in Lat. 45° 10' N., and Long. 124° 40' E.

白羊 Peh-yang, a country of the Hiungnu, or Turkic tribes.

裴獠 P'ei-láu, wild tribes in the island of Hainan.

毗騫 P'i-kien, Pegu, adjoining Burmah. See Peh-ngo.

毗舍耶 P'i-shié-ye, a name of Formosa. See T'ai-wan.

避暑山莊 P'i-shú-shan-chwang, the name of the Imperial palace and park at Jehol, 140 miles from Peking. It is delightfully situated in the midst of towering hills, and is enclosed by a great wall. Before the palace-gate there are inscriptions in Chinese, Manchu, Mongol, and Turkish, ordering passengers to dismount.

汴洲 Pien chau, a name of K'ai-fung fu in Honan in the Sung period, when it was the capital. See Pien-liang and Liang-chau.

汴京 Pien king, a name of K'ai-fung fu in Honan in the Han chau, Sui and T'ang periods. See Tung king. *Ta-liang* is a name referred to K'ai-fung fu.

汴梁 Pien-liang, the name of K'ai-fung fu under the Mongolian dynasty.

闢展 P'ih-chen, Pitshan, or Pidjan, a city of the Mahommedans, situated 760 *li* W. of Hamil, in Lat. 42° 45' N., and Long. 91° 10' E. See Shen-shen. This was formerly a chief city of the Uigurs.

拂林國 Pih-lin kwoh. See Fuh-lin kwoh.

檳榔 Pin-lang, the island of Penang. See Sin fau.

頻婆娑羅 P'in-p'o-so-lo, Rajagriha, the ancient capital of Magadha.

頻斯國 P'in-sz' kwoh, a country in Central Asia famed for its apples and fruits.

平壺島 P'ing-hu-t'au, the island of Firando, in Japan, which the Dutch left in 1640 for Desima, near Nagasaki. Here Koxinga was in all probability born of a Japanese mother. See Ching chi-lung and Wei-yang.

平江 P'ing kiang, a name of the Suchau region in Kiangsu province, during the Sung dynasty. It more strictly belongs to the district of Wu hien in this sub-department, of which it is still the official designation.

平陸 P'ing-luh, a district in Kiai chau (Shansi), identical according to some with Wan-shang, or with Chung-tu, the town of Lu, of which Confucius was chief magistrate. It afterwards belonged to the more northerly state of Ts'i. It is said by Amiot to have been the actual capital, as the name implies, of Lu. See Su-kü kwoh.

平順鎮 P'ing-shun chin, the Cohinchinese name of Tsiampa.

平泉州 P'ing-ts'iuen chau, or Pa-keu, a district city of Chihli, in the department of Ching-teh, beyond Jehol. It is the seat of extensive silk manufactures.

婆羅洲 P'o-lo chau, a modern term for the island of Borneo.

波羅門 Po-lo-mun, the Brahmins of India. The term is also applied to the Burmans.

波羅奈 Po-lo-nai, the city of Benares in India.

波羅斯 Po-lo-sz', a suggested name for Prussia, usually confounded with Austria. See Tsz'-ying, and Tan ying.

婆律國 P'o-luh kwoh, a country in the *Si Hai*, perhaps answering to Borneo, and yielding *lung-nau-hiang*, or Baros camphor. See Pa-tung. This drug is also called 羯婆羅香, Hoh-p'o-lo hiang. Is this a name for Borneo?

波那 Po-na, Poonah in India.

婆利 P'o-ni, the island of Borneo, a part of which is said by the natives of the island to have formerly belonged to China. It was once a dependency of *Tu-po kwoh* (Java). There is a modern state on the W. of the island called Pontiana. See Puh-ni and Wan-lai.

婆娑國 P'o-so kwoh, the country or the capital of Magadha. See Mo-kich-t'i kwoh.

波斯經教 Po-sz'-king kiau, the religion of Zoroaster, as embodied in the Persian Classic, the Zend Avesta. Occasionally the words Po-sz' may be understood as meaning Parsee. See Ho-shin kiau.

波斯國 Po-sz' kwoh, the country of Persia, the source of gum-resins, and many valuable medicines, said to have been introduced from thence to China.

亳 Poh, the capital of Kuh Kau Sin, answering to Yen-sz' hien, in Honan fu (Honan). This was also the capital of the Yin part of the Shang dynasty.

博羅 Poh-lo, the Chinese name of Marco Polo, the Venetian traveller. He was governor of a *lu*, or circuit, which included the city of *Yang-chau*, and 27 other cities, being part of the Mongol province which included Honan and Kiangpeh. See Chü-mih-fuh-sz'.

博羅特 Poh-lo-teh, a town in Kansuh.

博爾都噶爾亞國 Poh-rh-tu-koh-rh-ya kwoh, Portugal as written in recent Chinese documents.

薄宗城 Poh-tsung ching, a town and district in the S.E. part of Anterior Thibet, bordering on the Nu-í tribes which lie E. of Nepaul.

鄱陽湖 Poh-yang hu, the Poyang lake, so named from an island in it. See P'ang-li.

蒲昌海 P'u-chang hai, Lake Lop Nor in I'li, into which the Tarim flows, after receiving the Yarkand, Kashgar, Oksu and Khoten rivers. See Lo-pu-nau-rh.

蒲甘 P'u-kan, the city of Amarapura, a capital city of Burmah.

布魯沙布羅 Pu-lu-sha-pu-lo, Peshawur (or *Purushapura*, in Sanscrit), formerly the capital of Cabul. See Ngan-shih kwoh.

布魯特 Pu-lu-teh, the Bourouts, a vagrant Mahommedan tribe, bordering on Kashgar. They are divided into the eastern and western branches, and formerly sent a yearly tribute of horses to Ushi.

蒲類海 Pu-lui hai, Lake Barkul, near Chinsi fu. See Hiung-nu chung hai.

布尼 Pu-ni, a lake near Sansing in Kirin, through which the river Hourha runs (just as the Jordan flows through the Lake of Tiberias), and then joins the Songari.

布達拉城 Pu-tah-la ching, Budala, a name of H'lassa, the capital of Thibet, as containing the palace of the Dalai-lama, called *Potrang-marbu*, or "red town," on mount Budala, a little to the W. of the city proper.

布 特 哈 城 Pu-teh-ha ching, Putek in Hehlungkiang, or Tsitsihar, in Manchuria. The chief town of the district lies on the Nonni river, nearly opposite Merguen, and is the residence of the officer who has jurisdiction over the country between the W. bank of that river, and the Inner Hingngan range.

普 陀 山 P'u-to shan, the island of Puto, in the Chusan Archipelago.

濮 州 Puh chau, the capital of the Wei kingdom, in the Chau period, and now forming the departmental city of *Tung-chang fu* in Shantung.

渤 海 Puh-hai. This word primarily means an estuary or bay of the sea, but was applied to the Gulf of Liautung and to the Moh-hoh, a tribe of the Nu-chin dwelling near there. The term was also applied to the Yellow Sea, or the estuary of the Yellow River. In some recent Chinese works the Sea of Java, or the Sea of Borneo is called by this name. A division of the old principality or kingdom of Tsí-nan kwoh was called Puh-hai, including the present Li-tsin hien, Chen-hwa hien, Yang-sin hien, all in Shantung, and Nan-p'í hien in Pchchihli. These districts still enjoy this *pieh-ming*.

渤 泥 Puh-ni, the island of Borneo. See Po-lo chau and P'o-ni.

蒲 臺 P'u-tai, a place in the Tung-hai, where Ts'in Chi-hwang is said to have stalled his horses, with tethers of the Acorus plant, as the word P'u indicates.

本 地 Pun-ti, the "natives" of Canton province, as opposed, literally, to the immigrant Hakkas, or "settlers." The Puntis are said to have originally come from some neighbouring province.

蓬 萊 P'ung-lai, a place in Shantung, to which Yü's father was banished. This name is much used as a teashop sign in Hankow. See Kwan-t'i.

蓬 婆 城 P'ung-p'o ching, a garrison among the Turfan tribes.

盤 古 國 P'wan-ku kwoh, a kingdom in the China Sea, whose people were said to worship *P'wanku*, the Adam of the Chinese Genesis.

盤 盤 國 P'wan-p'wan kwoh, a country near the Kwanlun mountains, said to yield the best sulphur. This name is sometimes referred to Bantam in Java.

R

爾 撒 Rh-sah, the Mahommedan name for Jesus Christ. The words 耶 蘇 Ye-su, used in the Christian writings have become classical from their insertion in Kanghi's Imperial Dictionary.

薩拉齊 Sah-la-tsí, Sararchi, a *ting* district in the *Kweishu tau* in Pehchili.

撒馬兒罕 Sah-ma-rh-han. Samarcand (or Maracanda), the Mongol name of the ancient capital of Asia, containing the tomb of Timur. It is in Lat. 39° 56′ N., and Long. 66° 50′ E. Samarcand is now Russian territory, being the headquarters of the newly conquered district of Zariavshan. See Shié-mi-sz'-han and K'i-pin kwoh.

賽理木城 Sai-li-muh ching, Sairim, or Hanlemuh, a garrison subordinate to Ushi on the S. of the T'ien shan, in Lat. 41° 41′ N., and Long. 81° 58′ E.

三川 San ch'uen, the name of one of Ts'in Chi-hwang's forty prefectures, in Yu chau, or Honan.

三輔 San fu, the three principalities of Shensi, of which *Si-ngan fu*, *Fung-l*, and *Fu-fung* were the chief towns. See San ts'in.

三佛齊 San-fuh-tsí, a kingdom in the island of Sumatra. The piratical and comparatively civilized character of the people, agrees well with that of the Acheenese of the present day. Their houses are said to have been built on rafts or staging, on the waterside. The king bird of paradise, and the six-shafted variety came from there. The place called *Yu-t'o-li* has been referred to San-fu-tsí.

三韓 San-han, an old name of the region about the present Peking, included apparently in Liautung of that date, and answering to portions of Yü's province of K'i chau. It is placed in some Chinese works to the S.E. of Corea.

三河 San ho, the south, north, and west divisions of the Yellow River. See Si ho. There is a San-ho hien, in Shun-tien fu in Chihli province.

三合會 San-hoh-hwui, the Triad Society. See Ko-lau.

三教 San kiau, the three orthodox creeds, Confucianism, Buddhism and Tauism.

三國 San kwoh, the triarchy of "three kingdoms" of *Wei*, *Shuh* and *Wu*, which was formed at the close of the Eastern Han dynasty.

三笠 San-lih, or Sanlak, the island of Banca. See Kü-kiang.

三苗 San miau, the original stock of the Chinese aborigines, originally living in Wuchang fu, Yohchau fu, Kiukiang fu and portions of Nganhwui province, in the days of Yau, Shun and Yü They were removed, for insubordination, to *San Wei* in Kansuh. The *T'ang hiang*, who peopled Tangut and Thibet were descended from the San miau. See San wei.

三寶瓏 San-pau-lung, Sanpalang or Samarang in Java. Compare this name with San-fuh-tsí.

三山 San shan, a name of Fuhchau fu in Fukien province. See Yung ching.

三湘 San siang, a name of the present Hunan province. See Siang chung.

三姓城 San-sing ching, a garrisoned town in Kirin, situated at the junction of the Hurha branch with the Songari river. The resident officials have rule over the country of the Amur. The hunting tribes pay a tribute of peltry to the Chinese authorities.

三秦 San-ts'in, a division of the province of Kwanchung (Shensi), into three principalities in the Han period. See San fu.

三楚 San t'sú, three ancient divisions of Central China, commonly referred to Kingchau fu,

Hunan and Hupeh respectively, with a part of Honan. The word *T'su* is now commonly used as an equivalent for Hukwang.

三危 San wei, the scene of exile of the San miau, in the S.E. of the department of *Ngansi*, in Kansuh.

三吳 San wu, the region now known as Sangchau, Suchau and Huchau. See Wu chung.

僧格林沁 Sang-keh-lin-tsin. See Sang wang.

桑伽市 Sang-kia-shi, a kingdom in the Doab.

桑里 Sang-li, Sangri, or Samyé, a royal city near H'lassa. From this place formerly came the *Cordyceps Sinensis* (*Hia-ts'au-tung ch'ung*), a celebrated Chinese drug of great value in past time.

桑門 Sang-men, Buddhist priests. See Fau-tu and Sha-men.

僧王 Sang wang, or Sang-keh-lin-tsin, the Mongolian ally of the Chinese emperor, who commanded the army in the north of China in 1860.

沙州 Sha-chau, a name assigned by Pauthier to Tunhwang, a newly established district in Kansuh, to the S.W. of Ngansi. Biot places a small town, 80 leagues W. of Suhchau in Kansuh under this head, and a small town so named, of no importance, is placed in European maps a little to the S. of Tunhwang.

沙窒 Sha-chih, a kingdom in Oude.

沙人 Sha-jin, synonymous with Nung-jin.

莎車國 Sha-kü kwoh, an ancient name of Yarkand. See Yeh-rh-kiang.

沙瀝 Sha-lih, Macao Roads.

沙門 Sha-men, Buddhist priests. Shaman is a corruption of *Sramana*, a name of Buddha.

沙漠 Sha-moh, the desert of Gobi. See Ko-pih.

沙市 Sha-shi, a mart on the Yangtsz', 293 geographical miles from Hankow, and 3,380 *li* from Peking. There is water communication with the Han, by means of a canal, so that goods may be sent across the country to ports on the Han river.

山海關 Shan-hai-kwan, the point at which the Great Wall abuts upon the seacoast, on the western shore of the Gulf of Liautung. The town is in Lat. 40° N., and Long. 119° 50′ E. and consists of three distinct parts. It is now three or four miles from the sea, and is the point through which all goods for Manchuria and Corea must pass.

山戎 Shan-jung, a name of the Hiung-nu, in the time of the five emperors. See Hiung-nu.

山南 Shan-nan, the name of a large *tau*, south of one of the spurs of the Kwan-lun range and including parts of Honan, Hupeh and Shensi. It was divided into a west and an east portion. See Liu-kiu kwoh.

汕頭 Shan-tu, Swatow, the shipping port for the city of *Ch'au-chau fu*, a treaty-port in Kwangtung province, situated on the *Han kiang*. Swatow is distant some 180 miles from Hongkong.

上川山 Shang-ch'uen shan, the island of Sancian, miscalled St. Johns, a few miles W. of Macao, on which the body of Francis Xavier was temporarily interred. See Tsian shan.

上海 Shang-hai, the "higher sea" as distinguished from another, the "hia yang," or "lower sea." These were two of some eighteen estuaries which occupied the district S. of Sung-kiang. These were gradually silted up, but as it could still be "approached from the sea," the name of Shanghai was retained. The British settlement at this important treaty-port was founded in 1843. See Hu-tuh.

上黨山 Shang-tang shan, a hill in Shansi, or the S.W. of the old province of Yü, called K'i chau. The best ginseng is said to come from a valley near this hill. The best sesamum, and a drug called *tang-san*, probably a species of adenophora, are brought from this same district. Shang-tang was the name of one of Ts'in Chi-hwang's forty principalities, in the present Shansi province.

上都 Shang-tu, the Ciandu of Marco Polo, the summer residence of Kublai Khan. It was the old Mongol capital, subordinated by Kublai to Peking, which he called *Ta-tu.* See K'ai-p'ing. This name was also given to Si-ngan fu, as the capital of the T'ang dynasty.

上都河 Shang-tu ho, a branch of the Lwan river.

守禮 Shau-ni, Sheudi, the capital of the islands of Liu-kiu. See Na-pa.

首善 Shau-shen, a name given to Peking on Chinese maps, as the residence of the sovereign.

燒羊山 Shau-yang shan, a mountain in Turfan, yielding salt in crystals.

樀提 Sheh-t'i, the Chinese name for Jupiter, occurring in their "Classic of the stars."

陝州 Shen chau, a name of Shensi province, under the Tsin dynasty. See Tsin king. There is a sub-department of this name in Honan province.

檀戶 Shen-hu, the ancient serfs of China (Tsin, A.D. 280—404).

部善 Shen-shen, the ancient name of Pidjan, or Leu lan. See Pih-chen.

施備 Shi-pí, Cyamba or Tsiampa, referred to the modern Saigon. It is called *Luknooi* by the natives. See Chen ching.

社寮 Shié-liau, Palm Island, a small island near Kelung, in Formosa, formerly occupied by the Dutch.

舍彌斯罕 Shié-mi-sz'-kan, Samarcand. See Sah-ma-rh-kan.

蛇嶼 Shié-sü, Snake Island or Boomjes, a small island off the N. coast of Java, not far from Cheribon.

食火之國 Shih-ho-chi kwoh, a "country of fire-eaters" (Parsees?), to the south.

釋伽佯尼 Shih-kia-mau-ni, Shakyamuni, or *Shakya Sinha Gautama Buddha*, Gautama being the clan-name, and Buddha an appellation signifying the "Enlightened." See Ju-lai-fuh, and Mi-leh-fuh. The word *Sogomonibarkan* is used by Marco Polo for Buddha. Sinha signifies "lion." Muni stands for "monk." Barkan, or Bourkan, is a Mongol name for God.

釋教 Shih kiau, Buddhism, the Dissent from Brahminism, which became in A.D. 65 one of the three recognized creeds of China. See Fuh kiau.

舍利佛窆 Shih-li-fuh-chih, Sribodja, a kingdom washed by the Southern Sea.

十八省 Shih-pah sang, the "Eighteen Provinces," a common collective name for China. The British concession in Hankow is called *Shih-pah-tan*, "the eighteen pieces," so as to avoid inconvenient reference to its ownership or occupation.

實斑牛 Shih-pan-niu, a name given to Spain by the Chinese in the Straits.

碩般多城 Shih-pan-to ching, Shobando, a town and district in the north-eastern part of Anterior Thibet, W. of Tsiando.

深 海 Shin-hai, the "Deep Sea," the Pacific Ocean, in which *Sin-lo* is placed in Chinese maps. The great depth of this ocean is a tribute to the correctness of Chinese observation in this case.

神 國 Shin kwoh, or Shin-koku, "God-land," the dominions of the Mikado of Japan. See Hwang kwoh and Wei kwoh.

神 奈 川 Shin-nai-ch'uen, Kanagawa, a treaty-port of Japan.

身 毒 Shin-tuh, Sin-theu, or Sindhu, India or the country of the Sindhu, *the* river, the Indus. The name of India comes to us originally from the Persians who changed an initial *s* into *h*, so that *Sindia* became *Hindia* or *India*. This name has been referred by some to Scinde. See T'ien tuh.

盛 京 Shing king, or Liautung, is the name of the reigning dynasty for the metropolitan province of Manchuria, the Hanover of China. It is bounded N. by Inner Mongolia, N.E. and E. by Kirin. S.E. and E. by Corea, from which the river Yah-yuen divides it. S. by the gulf of Liautung, and S.W. by the Great Wall.

盛 京 本 城 Shing-king pun ching, the "head garrison of Shingking," or Shingking. Its Chinese name is commonly put down as Fung-t'ien fu, and its Manchu name as *Moukden*. It lies in Lat. 41° 50′ 30″ N., and Long. 123° 37′ E. See Fan-yang.

蜀 Shuh, an ancient tribe in Ching-tu fu, which has given its name to Sech'uen. The Ta Kiang is sometimes called *Shuh kiang*, or the Sech'uen river.

寂 昭 Shuh-chau, or Ziäku, a Buddhist priest who invented the Japanese syllabary of 48 syllables named after him. See Hungfah.

順 天 府 Shun-t'ien fu, the metropolitan prefecture, in which Peking is situated.

瑞 國 Shwui kwoh, the country of Sweden, sometimes called in Chinese works *Lin yin* or *Chen kwoh*. Norway is called Náu-wei kwoh.

西 番 Si-fan, the Kolo, or black-tented Thibetans residing near the sources of the Yellow River, and the N.W. of Sech'uen. They are regulated from Ta-ts'ien-lu, to which town they bring their tribute.

西 海 Si hai, a vague term applied to an inland sea which may have been either the Caspian or Mediterranean. Two western seas are spoken of in connexion with Ta-ts'in kwoh in such a way as to suggest that both seas were known to the Chinese by this name.

西 河 Si ho, an old name for a part of the Yellow River running between Shensi and Shanse.

西 和 州 Si-ho chau, a place in Kansuh, where Ts'in Chi-hwang commenced building the Great Wall.

西 胡 Si hu, "Western Barbarians," related to the Tungusic tribes of Eastern Asia. They are said to have had oxen, from which they cut off flesh with impunity, after the Abyssinian fashion.

西 羌 Si kiang, pastoral tribes from San miau, and identical with the Si hu. There is a *Kiang-li* spoken of as yielding sulphate of copper and other metallic salts.

西 傾 Si-king, a mountain in Kokonor. This was one of Yü's mountains, and is placed by some Chinese authors in Lin-t'au fu in Kansuh.

西 京 Si king, the "Western Capital," or Cochin China, as distinguished from Tonquin, or

Tung-king, the "Eastern Capital." See Hau-king. This name was given to Chang-ngan, or Si-ngan fu by the Chau dynasty.

西 蘭 Si-lan, or Ceram, one of the largest of the Molucca islands.

西 利 窐 Si-li-chih, } the island of Celebes.
西 利 窪 Si-li-wah, }

西 魯 Si-lu, a name of the region now forming Shansi province, as distinguished from Tung-lu, a name of Shantung.

西 彌 國 王 Si-mi-kwoh wang, the style of the Mahommedan ruler in Yunnan. See Tu-wan-siu.

西 南 夷 Si-nan-i, the Laos tribes betwen Siam, Burmah, and Annam.

西 安 府 Si-ngan fu, the chief city of Shensi, perhaps the Thinæ of Ptolemy, the *Singuy* of Marco Polo, and one of the great marts of China. It has frequently been the capital of the empire, and is celebrated as containing the site of the Nestorian Tablet, still preserved in a ruined temple outside the west gate of the city. See King-cháu fu, and Si-king.

西 寧 Si-ning, in Kansuh, the great western emporium of China. The governor of Tsinghai, or Kokonor, resides here. It is a *fu* city, in N. latitude 37°, and E. longitude 102°, and is the Jiling, or Siling of Major Montgomerie.

西 天 Si-t'ien, the western of the five divisions of India, as described in Chinese works. See Chung-t'ien-chuh.

西 藏 Si-tsang, Thibet or Tubet, or Bod. This large country extends from Lat. 27° to 33° or 35° N. It is divided into Anterior Thibet (*Ts'ien Tsang*), containing eight cantons, with H'lassa for its capital, and Ulterior Thibet (*Hau Tsang*), with its capital Teshu H'lumbu, and six cantons. Thibet is sometimes called *Wei-tsang* (衛 藏) in Chinese works, the Wei and Tsang corresponding to Anterior and Ulterior Thibet very nearly.

璽 䁑 國 Si-wan kwoh, a country in Thibet, near the Kwanlun range, yielding precious stones.

西 洋 Si yang, the "Western ocean," a name given to the sea beyond Cape Comorin, and sometimes applied to Europe, as in the Atlantic Ocean.

西 洋 古 里 Si-yang-ku-li or Kuli, Calicut. See Ku-li.

西 洋 國 Si-yang kwoh, the kingdom of Portugal, as the first of the countries of Europe known to China. Other countries were distinguished by peculiarities of flags, &c.

西 粵 Si-yueh, or Yueh-si, the province of Kwangsi.

相 Siang, one of the Shang capitals, now Chang-teh fu, in Honan.

湘 中 Siang chung, a name of the region now forming Hunan province. This is given by some as 湘 州, Siang-chau, a name of the Tsin period.

襄 河 Siang ho, a name of the River Han from its mouth to the city of *Siang-yang fu*, distant from Hankow some four hundred miles. Opposite this city is the mart of *Fan-ching*, standing in the same relation to Siang-yang as Hankow to Hanyang. Fan-ching is not half the size of Hankow.

象 郡 Siang-kiun, an old name of Jeh-nan in the time of Ts'in Chi-hwang.

箱 館 Siang-kwan, Hakodadi, a treaty-port of Japan.

湘潭 Siang-tan, in Hunan, Lat. 27° 52′ N., and Long. 112° 41′ E. It is one of the great tea and trading marts of China, situated on the river *Siang* or *Heng Kiang*, which runs into the southern part of the T'ung-ting lake.

小金川 Siau-kin-ch'uen, the country on the borders of Scch'uen, inhabited by a tribe of Miau-tsz', whose incursions and internecine warfare led to their extinction as a local tribe, under K'ien-lung about 1772. See Ta Kin Ch'uen.

小崑崙 Siau kwan-lun, the Alps or some range of mountains upon the Mediterranean shore.

小呂宋 Siau lu-sung, Manilla. See Lu sung.

小別山 Siau pieh shan, the celebrated hill in Han-chung fu, where the troops of Wu crossed the Han.

小西洋 Siau-si-yang, the Portuguese settlement of Goa. See Yin-tu-yang.

小東洋 Siau-tung-yang, the Sea of Japan. See Tung yang.

獫狁 Sien-li, the "crafty" northern "tykes," or "fiery dogs," near the N. bend of the Yellow River.

暹羅 Sien-lo, the kingdom of Siam, formed by the junction of 暹, *Sien*, and 羅斛, *Lo-hoh*, or *Lo-lo*. The whole of the Malayan Peninsula was once tributary to this state. See Ta-ni. In the T'ang time there was a Ch'ih t'u kwoh, probably identical with Siam.

鮮卑 Sien-pi, the Tungusic founders of the family who overcame the Wu-hwan king and reigned in China as the Liau dynasty. See K'i-tan. Dr. Oppert refers the Liau to a Mongolic origin.

息辣 Sih-lah, Singapore, or Salat, the Sada of ancient geographies. See Sin-kia-po.

錫蘭 Sih-lan, Junk-seylon near Penang.

錫蘭山 Sih-lan shan, Adam's Peak in Ceylon.

錫蘭山國 Sih-lan-shan kwoh, the kingdom of Ceylon, the *Lanka* of Buddhist works. See Sz-tsz'-kwoh. Lanka is written Lang-ka in Chinese books.

錫林郭勒盟 Sih-lin-koh-lih ming, one of the six *ming*, or corps of Inner Mongolia, living in the northern part of the country, beyond the Chau-wú-tah corps, and extending across the northern borders.

息垄 Sih-ti, or Sih-lam, Islam, a name used for Chinese Mahommedans in the Straits. See Moh-kia.

色仔年 Sih-tsz'-nien, the Seranis, a name given to the Portuguese in the Straits.

信州 Sin chau, an old name of Kwang-sin fu (Kiangsi), yielding ores of iron and copper.

新嘉坡 Sin-kia-po, Singapore, sometimes called Salat. See Sih-lah.

新羅 Sin-lo, a country, related to the San-han, in the Shin-hai, to the S.E. of Corea, and more than 500 *li* to the S.E. of Peh-tsí. It was called Sin-lu previous to the Sung period, and is also sometimes called Sz'-lo. Its sovereign, sometimes a female, annexed Peh-tsí to its own territory, during the T'ang dynasty, to whose sovereigns it presented tribute. This is probably the Loh-lang of Chinese writings. It is frequently mentioned in the Pen T'sau as yielding ginseng, seaweed, fruits, aconite, silver and other substances. This is also given as an old name of Chang-ting hien, in Fukien province.

星宿海 Sing-suh-hai, the name of the springs and pools at the source of the Yellow River, likened to constellations, as seen at a distance.

岫巖城 Siu-yen ching, a garrison in a district of the same name in Fung-t'ien fu, in Shingking, and subordinate to the head garrison of Shingking.

雪山 Siueh shan, the Himalaya, or "Snowy Mountains." This is to be distinguished from the Siueh ling. See Pa-yen-k'ch-lah.

雪山下 Siueh-shan-hia, the kingdom of Himatala in Turkestan.

宣化府 Siuen-hwa fu, the name given by the Kin and Manchu dynasties to the large trading prefectural city in Chihli, in Lat. 40° 38′ N., and Long. 115° E. It was a summer residence and subordinate capital of the Mongol emperors, under the name of Shang-tu, K'ai-ping and Siuen-teh. A little to the N.E. of the city is the site of Shang-kuh-ti, the city of a prefecture of that name, under T'sin rule.

朔方 Soh-fang, an ancient division of the empire, answering to Soh-p'ing fu (Shansi).

蘇方國 Sú-fang kwoh, the island of Sumbawa, yielding 蘇木, Sú-muh, or sappan-wood. See Li-ma.

疏和土 Su-ho-t'u, Surat, a kingdom in Hindostan, of the time of Baber.

徐戎 Su-jung, certain wild tribes of the time of Yü, living near the present province of Shantung. Su chau included portions of Nganhwui, Kiangsu and Shantung.

須句國 Su-kii kwoh, an old name of Tung-p'ing chau in T'ai-ngan fu (Shantung). This is also given as the same place as Chung-tu, the town in Shansi, of which Confucius was magistrate. There is evidently some confusion between this Tung-p'ing chau and Wan-shang (Shantung), a city of the Kin Tartars, identified by some with P'ing-luh, and still giving its name to a district. See P'ing-luh.

疎勒國 Su-leh kwoh, the ancient name of Kashgar, which sent lions as a present to one of the emperors of the After Han dynasty.

蘇祿 Su-luh, the territory of the Sultan of Sulu in the island of Borneo, including the Archipelago of the same name. He is said to send three ships laden with tribute once every five years to China. They bring articles of merchandise for sale, which are admitted free of duty.

蘇門答喇島 Su-mun-tah-lah t'au, the island of Sumatra. This is a modern name of what was called San-fuh-tsi. It was also anciently called Su-wan-tah-la.

蘇尼特 Su-ni-teh, the Sunnites, one of the largest tribes of Mongolia, dwelling from Cháhar to the N.W as far as Gobi, 500 li N. of Kalgan. .

肅愼氏 Suh-shin-shí, the Nu-chih or Tungusic ancestors of the Manchus, who derived their name of Kin from a tree which was said to produce gold.

綏定城 Sui-ting ching, or Tugnchuk, the chief town of the Tourgouths in Tarbagatai, lying to the W. of Kuldsha the capital of I'li.

碎葉 Sui-yeh, or Suïyip, one of the four states of Central Asia, tributary to China in the time of the T'ang dynasty.

綏遠城 Sui-yuen ching, in Kweisui tau in Shansi, the residence of the general commanding the Toumet tribe of Mongols. It lies a few miles E. of Kwei-hwa ching.

松 花 河 Sung-hwa ho, the Songari river, a large tributary of the Sagalien or Amur.

四 海 Sz' hai, the "four seas," said to be inhabited by the 九 夷, 八 狄, 七 戎, 六 蠻, amongst which foreigners are really included by the Chinese.

四 里 猫 Sz'-li-mau, Sourabaya in Java.

斯 眸 利 Sz'-me-li, Siberia. See Hi-kwoh.

四 明 Sz' ming, an old name of the district round Ningpo. This name is given to the well known Ningpo Joss-house at Shanghai.

獅 子 國 Sz -tsz' kwoh, the "Kingdom of Lions," Ceylon. This is simply a translation of *Sinhala* (Singhalese), the Sanscrit name for Ceylon. See Sih-lan-shan kwoh.

四 子 部 落 Sz'-tsz'-pu-loh, the Mongol tribe of Durban Keoukat, to the N. of Chahar.

四 瀆 Sz' tuh, the "four sluices" of China, the Yangtsz', the Yellow, the Hwai and the Tsí rivers. The Han, with other rivers, is sometimes mentioned as one of these four rivers, according to the dynasty. See Nu kiang.

T

大 川 Ta ch'uen, the Yellow River. See Hwang Ho.

大 法 國 Ta fah kwoh, France. The Chinese believe that the French were Buddhists until converted to the Romish creed. Just as the *Fuh* (Buddha) of the original name, Fuh-lang-si, embodied this idea, so the *Fah* (Dharma) of the term adopted by the French themselves, confirms this idea. The resemblance between Romanist and Buddhist practices must also have suggested it.

大 海 Ta hai, a term answering to the Sinus Magnus of Ptolemy, loosely applied to the Pacific Ocean, the China Sea, the Caspian Sea, and possibly the Mediterranean Sea.

大 漢 Ta han, a country to the E. of Wan-shin, of the same stock and first known to China in the Liang dynasty.

大 夏 Ta hia, a country more than 2,000 *li* to the S.W. of Ta-yuen kwoh and identified by Biot with Bactria. This country was named after the Dahæ, a warlike tribe from the eastern shores of the Caspian who invaded Bokhara and adjoining districts. Bactria, or Balkh, called *Po-lo* was termed the mother of cities, from its unrivalled antiquity and splendour. An affluent of the Yellow River near Lan-cháu bears the same name.

大 剛 國 Ta kang kwoh, Tagaung the ancient capital of Burmah. This is the same place as Pang-hang, or Paghan.

大 江 Ta kiang, the "Great River," the river Yang-tsz', 3,000 miles long.

大 金 Ta kin, the style of the Kin Tartars, ancestors of the present Manchu dynasty.

大 金 川 Ta kin ch'uen, a name given to one of the tribes of the mountainous districts of Sech'uen, identical with the Miau-tsz'. They were finally reduced, after fierce resistance, by the armies of K'ien-lung. The country is spoken of as *Liang Kin Ch'uen*, there being a *Siau Kin Ch'uen.*

大 境 Ta king, or Da-khin, the Deccan in India.

大 金 沙 江 Ta-kin-sha-kiang, the Brahmaputra River. See Ya-lu-tsang-pu.

大 沽 Ta ku, a important military post at a village on the southern side of the Peiho, near its mouth. It was at this point that the Yellow River anciently found its way into the Gulf of Chihli, probably by the channel of the Peiho.

大 理 府 Ta-li fu, a departmental city in Yunnan, in Lat. 25° 44′ N., and Long. 100° 21′ E. See Si-mi-kwoh wang. This is said by some to be the Yachi of Marco Polo.

大 呂 宋 Ta-lu-sung, Spain. See Shih-pan-niu.

打 彌 國 Ta-mi kwoh, a country on the "western borders."

大 明 海 Ta ming hai, the Pacific Ocean, whose "clear" and deep waters attracted the attention of the Chinese.

大 坭 Ta-ni, or Patani, a country in the Malay peninsula, a tributary of Siam. The southern part of this peninsula is sometimes spoken of as *Ko-lo-fu-sha.*

大 板 Ta pan, Osaka, a treaty-port in Japan.

大 別 山 Ta pich shan, the Hanyang hill, commonly called the *Kwei shan.* See Siau pieh shan.

打 牲 烏 拉 城 Ta-sang wu-la ching, a garrison in Kirin, a little to the N.E. of Kirin ula, in Lat. 44° 05′ N., and Long. 126° 10′ E.

大 食 Ta-shih, the Tajiks, of Persian origin, and of the Shüte sect, dwelling in *Tiau-chi* on the slopes of the Belur Tagh. They were confounded with the Arabs by the Chinese of the T'ang dynasty, and it is probable that more than one of the many countries conquered by them before they were subjugated by their Sunnite adversaries, were called after them. Christians in Persia were often called "Teizai," a name possibly connected with Ta-shih.

大 食 國 Ta-shih kwoh, Arabia. See T'ien-fang kwoh, and T'ien-t'ang.

大 西 洋 Ta-si yang, a name formerly applied to Europe, but now confined to Portugal.

大 西 洋 海 Ta si yang hai, the Atlantic Ocean.

打 箭 爐 Ta-tsien-lu, an important town in Sech'uen, in Lat. 30° 08′ 24″ N. Through this town the traffic between China and the tribes of Kokonor passes, and the officer who presides over nine tribes of the *Tu Sz'* resides here.

大 秦 Ta ts'in, the Roman empire, or some portion of it as Syria or Palestine. See Hai-si kwoh.

大 清 國 Ta-tsing kwoh, the official style of China, under the present dynasty.

大 都 Ta-tu, the name given to Peking by Kublai Khan, in 1272. He resided there in winter making *Ciando,* or *Shang-tu,* his summer residence. This name was sometimes given to

Siuen-hwa fu. See Siuen-hwa fu.

大同 Ta-t'ung, the Tanduc of Marco Polo, called also *Ta t'ung lu* during Mongolian rule. It was a part of Shansi and Pehchihli, which lay a little to the west of Peking, between the double portion of the Great Wall. It was considered the key of the empire. It is now the Ta-t'ung fu of Shansi, and was the seat of a mint, the coins issued from which are marked *T'ung.*

大萬谷落 Ta-wan-kuh-loh, a name of Kweichau in the Mongolian period.

大英國 Ta ying kwoh, Great Britain. England is sometimes spoken of as *Ying-kih-li.*

大越 Ta yueh, the national style of the former kings of Cochin China.

大月支 Ta-yueh-chi, the "Lunar Race" or Getæ, believed to be the Indo-Scythians of western writers. They conquered the country of the Indus, and their descendants are said by Klaproth to remain in these countries to this day as the Yuts, or Juts. See Wu-tien, and Yueh-ti.

大宛國 Ta-yuen kwoh, the "Country of great pasturages," identified with Kokand or Ferganah, fertile and populous from the flow of the Oxus and Jaxartes through it. Chinese works make Ta yuen 12,500 *li* from Si-ngan fu, and 2,000 *li* or more to the S.W. they place *Tu hia.* From this country many drugs and fruits were brought by Chang K'ien of the Han period.

達賴喇嘛 Tah-lai-lah-ma, the Dalai Lama, the Pope of Thibet.

塔爾奇城 Tah-rh-ki ching, Turk or Tartar city, a garrisoned town lying E. of I'li, on the I'li river. It is named from a mountain near it.

塔爾巴哈台城 Tah-rh-pa-ha-tai ching, Tarbagatai or Tashtava. An important garrison and town on the frontiers of I'li, in Lat. 47° N. The district of the same name is bounded N. by the Hassacks or Kirghis of Independent Tartary, and E. by Cobdo. It is inhabited by immigrant Tourgouths and other tribes from the steppes. 塔塔兒, Tah-tah-rh, is given as a name of a subordinate Turkic tribe, or Hiung-nu.

塔什干 Tah-shih-kan, Tashikan or Tasigan, a town of Western Tartary, in Lat. 43° 03′ N., and Long. 68° 45′ E. (Biot). This word 塔, tah may be written 搭. It probably refers to the Tartars or Tatars as 搭棚, Tah-p'ang, or "pitchers of tents."

韃靼 Tah-tan, the Tatars, a Mongolic race dwelling near the Lake Bonyir in Eastern Mongolia. The term has latterly been applied to Turkic or Turanian peoples, like the word Scythian.

韃靼 Tah-tsu, or 達達爾, Tah-tah-rh, the Tartars or Tungusic Manchus. The word is applied to Mongols, and is so mixed up with other opprobrius epithets, as 騷韃子, Sáu-tah-tsz', ("horsey Tartars"), that it is not used. 撻子, Tah-tsz' are perhaps the original characters intended to be used, and founded upon one of the Tartar forms of obeisance, in which the foot is struck upon the ground, and the gusue previously worn in front, is simultaneously thrown behind. The 泰赤烏, Tai-ch'ih-wu, 克列, K'eh-lich, and 塔塔兒, Tah-tah-rh are mixed up with the Mung-ku, who are said to have united to form the Yuen, or Mongolian nation. See Mung-ku.

太官 T'ai kwan, the Tycoon or Shiogoon, the Japanese generalissimo. See Kung fang.

太 南 T'ai-nan, or Dainam, the national style of the kingdom of Cochin China. See Ta yueh.

太 平 洋 T'ai-ping yang, the "Pacific Ocean," as named in foreign compilations.

太 子 Tai-tsz', the Emperor's heir, also called, 阿 哥 O-ko.

臺 灣 Tai-wan, the island of Formosa, with its capital city, Tai-wan fu, a treaty-port. This name of "Terrace Bay" was first applied to the group of islands on the western side of the present large island. The Japanese who made some efforts to settle there in 1620 called it *Taka Sago*, "high sand." It is divided into four hien and five ting districts so far as the Chinese possessions extend.

太 原 T'ai-yuen, the Great Plain of China. *T'ai-yuen fu* is the chief prefecture of Shansi.

蛋 Tan, a tribe of Miautsz' sometimes called *Tan-man*, or *Hu-i*. See Tan-kia.

蛋 家 Tan-kia, the boat-population of Canton, a distinct race of aborigines.

揮 國 Tan kwoh, a country to the N.E. of Ta-t'sin kwoh, on the road to which it lay. *Tana* is given by Pauthier as a name of Bombay.

擔 秋 Tan-mei, or Tan-mo-li-ti, the name of a country at the mouth of the Ganges, near the modern Tamlook.

淡 水 Tan-shwui, Tamsui, or Tan-shwui-ting, the best port in Formosa, in Lat. 25' 10' N.

丹 丹 國 Tan-tan kwoh, a country of India to the S.E. of the department of Tsin-chau. The name of *Tan-tan* is used for Bantam in Java.

單 于 Tan-yu, or Shan-yu, the name of the king or of the kingdom of the Hiung-nu.

單 鷹 Tan-ying the "single eagle," a term applied to the flag and kingdom of Prussia.

宕 州 Tang chau, a name of Tangut given by Pauthier. There was also in Tangut a Tang-chang.

登 州 府 Tang-chau fu, the prefectural city and port in Shantung, inserted in the treaty of 1858, but exchanged for the town of *Yen-tai*, confounded with *Chi-fau*, or Chefoo, a harbour in the same bay. See Lai-tsz' kwoh.

黨 項 T'ang-hiang, a tribe descended from the San Miau, giving their name to the next.

當 享 Tang-hing, a part of Kansuh, answering to the present *Fuh-kiang hien*.

騰 格 里 Tang-keh-li, the Tengri Tagh or celestial mountains. See T'ien shan.

唐 努 烏 梁 海 T'ang-nu Wu-liang-hai, one of the districts dependent on Uliasutai, inhabited by the Wulianghai, or Uriankai tribes, and the Kalkas and Tourgouths of the Tang-nu mountains. This tract of country lies N.E. of Cobdo, N. of the Sannoin and Dzassaktu Khanates, and is divided from Russia by the Altai mountains. The government of these tribes is administered by 25 subordinate military officers.

唐 山 T'ang-shan, the name of a mountain in Chihli. This is also a common name for China in general use in Java, the Straits, the Sandwich Islands and wherever Chinese emigrants, called *T'ang-jin*, are located. The name arose from the fact that the first settlers in Java left China during the T'ang period.

騰 越 州 Tang-yueh chau, Moulmein in Burmah.

投 和 T'au-ho, a place in the China Sea named after its king, and answering to Mindoro.

島 夷 T'au-i, a name of the wild inhabitants of Liautung, Tarakai, Yesso, and perhaps Japan.

刀筋教 Tau-kin-kiau, or Tiau-kin-kiau, the "sect which cuts away the sinew," a Chinese name for the Jews. See T'ien kiau and Kiu kiau.

陶塗 T'au-t'u, a Tartar country yielding excellent horses called after this northern region. Their principal value was their power of making long journeys.

特穆眞 Teh-moh-chin, Temugin, commonly called Genghis (the greatest) Khan.

地中海 Ti-chung hai, the Mediterranean Sea, as named in a modern Chinese work, the *Kau-hau-mung-kieu*, to which those who desire to coin new geographical terms would do well to resort.

條支 Tiau-chi, a country bordering on the Caspian Sea, mentioned in connection with the journey westward of *Kan Ying*, a general under the orders of *Pau chau*. This country was inhabited in all probability by Tajiks, "traders" of Persian and Arabian extraction.

鐵嶺縣 Tieh-ling hien, a district of Fung-t'ien fu in Shingking, in Lat. 42° 25′ N., and Long. 123° 45′ E.

鐵帽子王 Tieh-mau-tsz'-wang, a title for bravery given to Mongolian and Manchurian princes, reminding one of the order of the "Iron Crown" of Lombardy. See Tieh-muh-er.

鐵門關 Tieh-men-kwan, the "Iron-gate Pass," in Lat. 37° 35′ N., and Long. 118° 12′ E. is the port of the Yellow River, some twenty miles from the point where the river taking possession of the bed of the Ta-tsing river, pours itself into the Gulf of Pehchihli, as of old.

鐵木兒 Tieh-muh-er, Timur, the Lame. The word "timur" in the Tchagatai (Tartar-Turkish) dialect signifies "iron," as does the Chinese "*tieh.*" It is probable that the title of *Tieh-mau* mentioned above is derived from Timur.

天朝 T'ien-chau, the "Heavenly dynasty," or the empire and sovereignty of China.

天主教 T'ien chü kiau, the Romish religion. It was sometimes called *Slah-tsz'-kiau*, or the "Religion of the cross."

天竺教 T'ien chuh kiau, the "Syrian religion," a name for the Jewish faith in China. See T'ien-tuh.

天竺國 T'ien chuh kwoh, Syria and India are included under this name originally applied to India only. See T'ien-tuh. This country was divided into five kingdoms by the Chinese, corresponding to the five *fang*, or points. See Chung-t'ien kwoh.

天方國 T'ien-fang kwoh, a name for Mecca and Arabia Felix or Yemen.

天下 T'ien hia, or *P'u-t'ien-hia*, the Chinese Empire, as distinguished from *Chung kwoh*, the "Mother country," Honan, &c.

天河 T'ien ho, the Milky Way. See Yun-han.

祆教 T'ien kiau, or *Heen kiau*, the Jewish faith. See Ts'ing-chin kiau.

天國 T'ien kwoh, the rebel kingdom proclaimed in 1851 by *Hung Siu-ts'iuen*, the *Tai-p'ing wang*. The words 天朝, *T'ien chau*, and 承平, *Ch'eng p'ing* are required to be used in all essays and documents, where T'ien kwoh and Tai-p'ing used to be spoken of. See Yueh fei.

滇國 Tien kwoh, one of the "contending states," answering to Yunnan province.

天山 T'ien shan, the 'Celestial mountains," the Tengri Tagh of the *Tu-kiueh* (Turks), and Hiung-nu. The mean parallel of latitude oscillates between 40° 40′ and 43° N. latitude. .

The range is eight times as long as the Pyrenees, is volcanic, and rich in metalliferous ores. See Nan shan.

天 山 南 路 T'ien shan nan lu, the "circuit south" of the T'ien shan, between this range and the Kwanlun mountains. It is called Sin Kiang or Ihwi Kiang.

天 山 北 路 T'ien shan peh lu, Songaria, the "circuit north of the T'ien shan," lying between Long. 72° and 88° E., and Lat. 42° to 49° N.

天 堂 T'ien-t'ang, Arabia Felix. See Ta-shih kwoh.

天 津 T'ien tsin, the port of Peking. This is also the name of the constellation Cygnus.

天 子 T'ien tsz', the Emperor of China. These two characters signifying the "Son of Heaven," are identical with those given for the Sora Mikado of Japan, who claims equal honours with the Chinese emperor.

天 都 T'ien-tu, an imaginary place in the Southern Sea, or the coast of Fukien, connected with the Queen of Heaven, or with Kwan-yin. Nunneries have this name in some cases.

天 毒 T'ien-tuh, India. See Chau-sien-t'ien-tuh. This character is derived from Shin-tuh (身 毒), which, in the judgment of some, primarily stood for Scinde, as it is placed to the S.E. of Ta Hia, or Bactria by Chinese writers.

天 篤 T'ien-tuh, India. This name has given rise to some confusion. This tuh has been exchanged with the tuh of the previous name, and the tuh of the present term having been written in the grass character 竺, has given rise to a third term 天 竺, T'ien chuh for India, not Syria.

狄 Tih, the red and white Tykes, or "fiery dogs," at the northern bend of the Yellow River. See Sz' hai.

迪 化 州 Tih-hwa chau, in Songaria, sometimes called Urumtsi. It is now attached to the province of Kansuh, and divided into four districts.

廷 遼 Ting-liau, a region bordering on Corea.

多 維 蠻 To-lo-man, tribes in Kwangsi, and between that and Annam.

多 倫 諾 爾 To-lun-noh-rh, Tolon nor, "Seven lakes," the great entrepot of the trade of the Sunnites, on the southern slope of the In Shan.

層 檀 T'siang-tan, an island in the Flores Sea, yielding fragrant woods.

齊 州 Ts'i chau. See Tsi-nan fu.

齊 國 Ts'i kwoh, an ancient state in Shantung, including Tsi-nan fu, Ts'ing-chau fu and Wei hien.

濟 隴 城 Tsi-lung ching, Dsilung, a district and town on the southern frontier of Ulterior Thibet, and W. of Nielam.

濟 南 府 Tsi-nan fu, the premier fu and capital of Shantung, also called 齊 州, Tsi-chau. This was called Ts'i-nan kwoh in the beginning of the Han dynasty.

齊 地 Ts'i-ti, an old name of Yang-kuh hien (Tung-o-hien of the Han), Shantung.

齊 齊 哈 爾 城 Tsi-tsi-ha-rh ching, the large town of T sitsihar hotun in Hehlungkiang, the third division of Manchuria, often called Tsitsihar. It lies on the Nonni branch of the Songari river, in Lat. 47° 20' N., and Long. 123° 30' E. It is the seat of the provincial government, and a place of some trade.

將軍 Tsiang-kiun, the Chinese and Japanese name for the Shiogoon. See T'ai-kwan.

譙 山 Tsiau-shan, the island miscalled "Silver Island," two miles below Chinkiang, on the Yangtsz'. The Chinese characters signify "Watch-tower mount," all islands being described as hills under the term 山, *shan*, or 島, *tau*.

僬 僥 氏 Tsian-yau-shi, a tribe of dwarfs on the south-west of China in the T'ang time.

前 山 寨 Tsien-shan-chai, the military station of Casa Branca, near Macao, in the Canton prefecture.

前 藏 Ts'ien-tsang, Anterior Thibet, sometimes called Wei (衛). See Wei-tsang.

且 末 Ts'ie-moh, a country in Central Asia, yielding excellent grapes.

七 洲 Ts'ih-chau, the "Seven islands, or Paracel reefs in the China Sea.

秦 Ts'in, the name given to China before the dynasty of that name. It occurs in the Laws of Menu, B.C. 1000. This name was probably the origin of the Sinæ or Thinæ of the ancients.

秦 中 Ts'in-chung, the province of Shensi.

秦 州 Ts'in chau, one of the principalities or prefectures of the Ts'in time, with Singan fu for its capital under the name of Shang-tu. It is now the name of a sub-department in Kansuh.

秦 境 Ts'in-king, an old name of Shensi province.

晉 地 Tsin-ti, the name given in the Chau period to Tai-yuen fu and P'ing-yan-fu in Shansi province. There was a 晉 城, Tsin-ching, in Tseh-chau (Shansi) also during the Chau dynasty, and the capital of the usurpers 韓, Han, 魏, Wei, and 趙, Chau.

清, Ts'ing, the Manchu "pure" dynasty, and its language. See Ta-ts'ing kwoh.

青 州 Ts'ing-chau, one of Yü's nine provinces, including the present Shantung, with parts of Liautung and of Corea.

清 眞 教 Ts'ing-chin kiau, the "doctrine of purity and truth," This is the legend written over the door of the Jewish sinagogue at K'ai-fung fu. The term is also used for Mahommedan mosques (清 眞 寺). See Yih-tsz'-loh-nieh-tien.

晴 川 Ts'ing-ch'uen, a name of the Hanyang city and neighbourhood. There is a 晴 川 閣, Ts'ing-ch'uen koh, at the foot of the Hanyang hill, facing the 黃 鶴 樓, Hwanghoh-lu on the Wuchang side.

青 齊 T'sing-tsí, a poetical name of Shantung, compounded of that of two of the principal prefectures, Ts'ing-chau fu and Tsí-nan fu. This was formerly a favourite way of building up names of provinces.

青 海 Ts'ing-hai, the "Azure Sea," or Kuku nor, (commonly written Kokonor), the "Blue lake," a name for what is properly a part of Mongolia, as inhabited by Mongols of the Tourgouth, Hoshoit and Kalkas tribes. It is sometimes called *Si-fan*, *Si-yih*, *Surfan* or *Tangut*. Several large lakes are found writhin its limits, after the largest of which it is named

泉 州 府 T'siu'en-chau-fu, the city of Chinchew near Amoy. It is the Taitun of Marco Polo.

祚 Tsoh, a tribe of I' on the S.W. near the Yen-yuen hien (Sech'uen) of the present day.

宗 喀 城 Tsung-keh ching, Dsunggar, a town and district of Ulterior Thibet W. of Dsilung, near the southern frontier.

總 理 衙 門 T'sung-li ya-men, the "Board of Control" at Peking, commonly called the "Foreign Office," a name more appropriate for the Li-fan-yuen, which see.

葱 嶺 T'sung ling, the "Onion" or Belur tagh range of mountains, including the Karakorum mountains, together forming the connecting links between the T'ien shan and the Kwan-lun ranges.

崇 明 縣 Tsung-ming hien, the district formed during the Yuen dynasty upon the deltoid island at the mouth of the Yangtsz'. It is 32 miles in length and from 5 to 10 miles in breadth, and has been formed since the 14th century by upheaval of the coast-line and alluvial deposits. It supports a numerous population. The little town has been removed some five different times from the freaks of the ocean. The island is sometimes called *Kiang-sheh*, "river's tongue," and *Hai-men*, "door of the sea."

紫 禁 城 Tsz' kin ching, the "forbidden city of the ruddy dawn," the Imperial residence in the *Nui ching* or Tartar city, forming the northern portion of Peking. It is about two miles in circumference. Red is an imperial colour, and has been changed with black or yellow, according as the fortunes of the imperial families or founders of dynasties have come under the influences of fire, water or earth.

紫 塞 Tsz' seh, the "red boundary," a name of the Great Wall, from the red colour of the earth used in many places for its construction. See Wan-li-chang-ch'ing and Kiu-seh.

孖 鷹 Tsz'-ying, or Ma-ying, a name applied to Austria from the double eagle on its flag.

吐 番 Tu-fan, the Turfans, or the Thibetans. See T'u-peh-teh and Wu-sz'-tsang.

土 黑 特 Tu-heh-teh, the name of a tribe of Mongols, living N.W. of Shingking.

吐 谷 渾 Tu-kuh-hwan, a Tungusic tribe, originally in Liautung, but who migrated to Yin shan in Kokonor, in the Si Tsin time.

都 江 Tu kiang, a name of the Yangtsz', or rather of the Min kiang, formerly considered by the Chinese as the main stream of the Ta Kiang.

塗 林 T'u-lin, a town in Ngan-si, or Cabul, visited by Chang K'ien of the Han dynasty.

土 魯 番 廳 Tu-lu-fan ting, the *ting* district of Turfan, now included in the district of Barkul, or Chinsi fu in Kansuh. The chief town is situated on the confines of the Great Desert, south of the *T'ien shan*, in Lat. 42° 40′ N. and Long. 90° 48′ E. This district is noted for its excellent wool, grown on the *T'ien shan* slopes. It was formerly called *Ho chau*, the "fire district," from its volcanic character. There is still an active volcano midway between the meridians of Turfan and Pidjan. See Ho chau.

土 默 特 Tu-meh-teh, the Toumets of Kuku koto, a tribe of Mongols living N. of Shansi, and N.E. of the Ortous. They are not included in Inner Mongolia, but nominally in Shansi, and governed by a general residing at Suiyuen ching. There are Toumets in the north of Pehchihli.

圖 伯 特 T'u-peh-teh, or Tu-po, a name of Tubet or Thibet. It was so called from the *Tu*, a foreign tribe which overran the present country of Thibet in the 6th century. See Wu-sz'-(sang.

閣 婆 國 Tu-p'o kwoh, a kingdom in Java whose capital was near Bantam, and extended its rule over the adjacent islands. This has possibly been confounded by the Chinese with the ancient kingdom of Taprobane, assigned to Ceylon or Sumatra.

都 波 羅 門 Tu-po-lo-men, the country of the Turcomans or Tajiks. This is referred by some to Kerman, now an eastern province of Persia, celebrated for the Kermanese wool of its sheep and goats, thick and silky, but not capable of taking that brilliant colour which gives the charm to the genuine Cashmere shawl, made from a wool called *pushm*. Kerman is the ancient Carmania.

土 爾 扈 特 部 Tu-rh-hu-teh pu, the Tourgouths. This Mongol tribe resides principally in Kokonor, to the S. of the "Azure Sea," and with the Hoshoits, Kalkas and other tribes around this sea, or lake, are arranged under 29 standards. They are controlled by a Manchu general residing at Sining fu in Kansuh. There are also the Tourgouths of the Tangnu mountains in western Mongolia, and a small band in Songaria. A large number emigrated from Russia into China in 1772, and are located in Tarbagatai and Cobdo. They had been originally driven out of Cobdo by Arabdan, Khan of the Songares, and were induced to return by imperial invitation.

都 兒 格 Tu-rh-keh, Turkey as named in Japanese maps. The Chinese equivalent is *Tu-rh-ki*.

杜 爾 伯 特 Tu-rh-peh-teh, the Tourbeths or Durbeths, a tribe of Mongols living in the extreme east of Inner Mongolia, on the Nonni river.

杜 文 秀 Tu-wan-siu, the name of the Mahommedan ruler in Yunnan. He reigns at Ta-li fu on the borders of Burmah. See Si-mi-kwoh wang.

突 何 Tuh-ho, the "turbaned" tribes of Turkestan.

突 何 羅 Tuh-ho-lo, Turkestan, or "the land of the turbaned race."

突 厥 Tuh-kiueh, the name of the Turkic tribes or Hiung-nu during the T'ang time. They wore helmets, as their name signifies, and were skilful in working in iron. Their country included the whole range of the Altai mountains, and stretched from the Amur river to the Caspian sea.

獨 石 口 Tuh-shih k'au, a pass in the Great Wall, in Lat. 41° 19' 20" N.

獨 逸 Tuh-yih, a name for Austria on Japanese maps, as one of the *Luh-ti kwoh*, or "Six despotic empires" of the world.

頓 遜 Tun-sun, a place to the S. of Burmah, answering to Tenasserim.

沌 陽 Tun-yang, a name of the city of Hanyang. See T'sing-ch'uen.

東 海 Tung hai, the "Eastern Sea," off the south-east coast of China. This was formerly the name of the present Yen-ching hien in Shantung.

東 海 道 Tung-hai-tau, the Tocaido or great military highway in Japan, extending from Nagasaki to Hakodadi.

東 胡 Tung-hu, the Tungusic tribes of Manchuria and Siberia. The word *hu* may have had the same origin as the word "manna," "what is it"? Foreigners bringing new and strange things, puzzled the Chinese as to where they came from. Hence the word *hu*, signifying how? whence? or what? may have come to be extended to all foreigners and their manufactures or natural productions. Colocynth and linseed among medicines, and parsnips, walnuts, onions and pepper, articles of food, have this prefix of *hu*.

東京 Tung king, the "Eastern Capital," or Tonquin, to distinguish it from *Si King*, or Cochin China. The kingdom of Tonquin existed as a separate state in the time of Marco Polo, who calls it *Aniu*. Its capital is Kesho. K'ai-fung fu is sometimes spoken of as Tung-king. See Tung king ching.

東京城 Tung king ching, in Shingking, a garrison subordinate to Shingking pun ching. This was the old capital of Liautung under the Ming rule, when that province was much smaller than the present Shingking. Some of this province had previously included Corea, and parts of the old province of *Tsing-chau*, portions of which are now submerged by the alterations of the sea-level. See Ts'ing-chau and Yu-t.

潼關 Tung kwan, an important town and fortress in Lat. 34° 50′ N. and Long. 110° 05′ E. at the southern bend of the Yellow River. It is called the key of Shensi province.

東魯 Tung-lu, the name of the present department of *Yen-chau fu* in Shantung, but formerly applied to the whole province. See Si-lu.

東苗 Tung-miau, an old name of Shantung.

東南 Tung-nan, a distinguishing name applied to the Sung dynasty from its geographical position.

東寧 Tung-ning, the name of Tai-wan fu, a treaty-port in Formosa, as the capital of Koxinga.

東阿縣 Tung-o hien, the old name of *Yang-kuh hien* in Shantung, during the Han period, from whence comes the *O-kiau*, or ass's glue, as it is called by some. It is said to be made from the water of a well which contains a gelatinous principle, like that of Barèges in France, and is used as a mild purgative and deobstruent. Deer's horn and cow's hide are often added to sophisticate the glue, which is reputed to be nourishing and astringent. See A-yih.

東浦寨 Tung-p'u-chai, Cambodia. See Chin-lah.

洞庭湖 T'ung-ting hu, the T'ung-ting lake in Hunan (a district *lu* under the Sung), the largest of the five great lakes of China. The old province of *Hukwang*, formed under the Mongols, was redivided into *Hunan* ("south of the lake"), and *Hupeh* ("north of the lake"), as a more convenient arrangement, or rather a return, necessitated by the position of the dangerous lake, which especially interfered with attendance upon the literary examinations at the capital, Wuchang. Hupeh province is often called Ngoh sang. See Ngoh-chu.

東土 Tung t'u, a Mahommedan name for China. See Ch'ih-ni.

同文館 T'ung-wan kwan, the name of the schools connected with the *Tsung-li yamen*, in which the Chinese and Manchus are taught European languages.

東洋 Tung yang, the "Eastern Ocean," or the Pacific Ocean, including the Yellow Sea, the straits of Corea and the Sea of Japan. This name is often applied to Japan and the Japanese. This name also occurs as the old name of *Ning-teh hien* in Fukien province.

東粵 Tung-yueh, Canton province. See Yueh, and Yueh-tung.

U

嶼 城 Ǔ ching, a fortified town on an island placed near Batavia, on Chinese maps of the Straits, and sometimes called Onrust.

翁 牛 特 Ung-niu-teh, thé Ouniots, a tribe of Mongols, living on the borders of Pehchihli, N. of the Hifung gate in the Great Wall.

W

外 番 Wai-fan, the foreign tribes in Mongolia, I'li, Cobdo and Kokonor. These were also spoken of as Fan-fuh.

外 夷 Wai-í, the external barbarians including all foreign countries. See Nui-í.

汶 江 Wan kiang, a name of the Yang-tsz'-kiang, near the prefectural city of Kwei-chau in Sech'uen. This is to be distinguished from the Wan-ho, a river in Shantung.

萬 古 屢 Wan-ku-lu, Bencoolen in Sumatra. See Wang-kiu-li.

文 萊 Wan-lai, a name applied to a part of the island of Borneo. See P'o-lo kwoh. Several nations of "marked" savages were placed by the Chinese to the E. of their empire. See Wan-shin.

萬 里 長 城 Wan-li-chang-ching, the Great Wall of China. See Tsz'-seh.

汶 上 Wan shang, the name of a district of Kwan-chau fu (Shantung) of the present time. It received its name from the Kin Tartars. It is referred, in the *Kwang-yü-ki*, to the situation of Chung-tu, of the state of Lu, and is made to correspond with the districts of

P'ing-luh, Peh-tsí, and Loh-p'ing of the Han dynasty. There is evidently some confusion with Tung-p'ing chau. See Chung-tu, P'ing-luh, Tung-p'ing chau, and Su-ku kwoh.

文身 Wan-shin, a country of "marked" savages more then 7,000 *li* to the N.E. of Japa: It was rich in precious stones and metals. Tamulo-Japanese nations on the E. for ages afflicted the Chinese.

萬水朝東大海 Wan-shwui-chau-tung-ta-hai, a Chinese name or expression, applied to the Pacific Ocean, from the tendency of the current of the sea outside the Japan islands to the E. See Wei-lu.

溫宿 Wan-suh, an ancient name of Aksu in Chinese Turkestan.

萬丹 Wan-tan, Bantan in Java. See Tan-tan kwoh.

萬全都 Wan-ts'iuen-tu, the Ming style for what is now Siuen-hwa fu (Chihli). See Siuen-hwa fu.

溫泉 Wan-ts'iuen, an old name of Kansuh.

溫都斯但 Wan-tu-sz'-tan, a Chinese name of Hindostan. See Han-tu-sz'-tan.

王仁 Wang-jin, or Wonin, a descendant of Kau-tsu, the first emperor of the Han dynasty, who accompanied some Japanese from Corea, and introduced the Chinese language and literature into Japan.

望久里 Wang-kiu-li, Bencoolen in Sumatra. See Wan-ku-lu.

王舍 Wang shié, Rajagriha, a royal city on the Ganges.

王庭 Wang-ting, the court of the sovereign of the Tuk-kiueh, or Turks, held at Urumtsi, during the 5th century. See Wu-lu-moh-tsí.

倭國 Wei kwoh, or Wa koku, the name used by both the Chinese and Japanese for Japan. Wei is read *Yamato* in Japanese books. See Jeh-pun kwoh. A distinction is sometimes made in ancient books, between Jeh-pun kwoh and Wei kwoh.

尾閭 Wei-lu, a name for the sea to the E. of Japan and the Liukiu islands, so-called from the easterly current setting up here, as described in Chinese works. This is also sometimes called Kuro Siwo, "Black Stream."

渭南 Wei-nan, a name of Shensi province in the early Han period.

倭奴 Wei-nu, the Japanese. This name was used in the Ming period by Chinese women to terrify their children, so fearful and frequent were the invasions of these Normans of the East upon the whole coastline of China. See Wei-tsz', and Wei-yang.

衛藏 Wei-tsang, Thibet. See Si-tsang

倭子 Wei-tsz', an opprobrious term first used for the Japanese, after their pretended subjection, and now commonly applied by the Pekingese to foreigners in general. It is sometimes confounded by foreigners with the more definite *yang-kwei-tsz'*.

尉頭國 Wei-t'u kwoh, an old name of Ushi, in Chinese Turkestan. See Wu-shih ching.

渭陽 Wei-yang, a name referred to Japan, or some prince of the country, mentioned in the account of Koxinga in the Tai-wan-chi.

維揚 Wei-yang, a name of Yang-chau fu during the middle period of the Ming. It was subsequently changed to the latter. It is one of the best traits of the Manchu emperors, that they refrained from all wanton change and confusion of old names.

吳 Wu, a kingdom including in Confucius's time the N. of Chekiang (Hu-chau, Yen-chau and Kia-hing chau) province and the southern part of Kiangsu. In the triarchy of the San kwoh it included the San Kiang provinces, or 61 prefectures. The kingdom of Wu was merged into that of the conquering state of Yueh in the same provinces.

烏稏國 Wu-c'ha kwoh, Orissa in India.

烏萇國 Wu-chang kwoh, the Buddhist country of Uchang ("the garden"), near the Punjaub.

吳州 Wu chau, an old name of Jau-chau fu, in Kiangsi.

烏運國 Wu-ch'i kwoh, a country in Asia Minor, or Eastern Europe, mentioned in connexion with 大秦, Ta Ts'in, or Ta Ts'in kwoh, commonly understood to refer to the Roman empire. It is however just possible that Greece, or Asiatic colonies, under the name of Achaia, is indicated by this name. Otherwise Greece was unknown to China.

五鎮 Wu chin, a term misinterpreted as referring to the "five marts" of China. There are very many chin, or "marts" in China, but four, and not five, are commonly spoken of as remarkable, rather than as simply large trading towns. These are Fuh-shan (Canton), King-teh chin (Kiangsi), Han-chin, or Hankow (Hupeh), and Chü-shien chin (Honan). The Wu chin, were the "five guardian hills" of the ancient empire in Yü's time,—namely 沂山, Ni shan (Shantung) on the E., 會稽山, Hwui-k'i shan (Chekiang), on the S. 霍山, Hoh shan (Nganhwui), in the centre, 吳山, Wu shan (Shensi), on the W. and 醫無閭山, I'-wu-lu shan (Shingking).

烏朱穆桑 Wu-chu-moh-ts'in, the Oudjamuchin, a tribe of Mongols living south of the desert, near the Shingngan mountains, S. of Hurunpir.

吳中 Wu-chung, the region now divided into the three departments of Sang chau, Su chau and Hu chau. It was called Wu kiun and San Wu.

巫咸國 Wu-hien kwoh, a country of serpent-charmers near the Wu shan, given to Fung-shuh, the body-physician of the emperor Yáu.

烏桓 Wu-hwan, a country on the "Western borders," peopled by a Tung-hu tribe, which aided in driving away the Hiung-nu during the Eastern Han period, but were themselves exterminated by the Liau.

無人島 Wu-jin t'au, the Bonin or Arzobispo Islands, supposed to be uninhabited, as the name signifies.

吳郡 Wu kiun, the region now divided into the three departments of Sangchau, Suchau and Huchau, in Kiangsu and Chekiang. See Wu chung.

烏喇忒 Wu-lah-tih, the Urats, a tribe of Mongols living in the valley of Kadamal, N. of the Yellow River, and E. of the Ortous. They are probably the Horiads of Marco Polo.

烏蘭察布盟 Wu-lan-chah-pu ming, one of the six corps of Inner Mongolia, living in the south-west, towards Kansuh and Shensi, outside of the Great Wall.

烏理雅蘇臺 Wu-li-ya-su-t'ai, Uliasutai, the city of the "Poplar Grove," in the Khanate of Sannoin, lying N.W. of the Selenga river in a well-cultivated and pleasant valley. It is the residence of a high officer who superintends the Ulianghai tribes, and the

Mongolian tribes living in Cobdo and the western portion of Mongolia.

武 林 Wu-lin, a name applied to Hangchow, and to Chekiang province, from a range of hills near Hangchow.

烏 魯 穆 齊 Wu-lu-moh-tsi, Urumtsi, a town in Songaria, on the N. of the T'ien shan, now included in Kansuh. It was the residence of the Tuh kineh sovereigns of the 5th century, and is in Lat. 43° 45′ N. and Long. 89° E. Exiled criminals are sent here to till the soil, and the nomadic tribes have been successfully encouraged to settle in this ungenial district. See Tih-hwa chau.

烏 魯 蘇 木 丹 Wu-lu-su-muh-tan, a town or post at the point of junction of the Humari and Sagalien rivers.

烏 蠻 Wu man, the Karens, or "black savages" of Kauting, or Caraian. See Ngai-lau-i. Kara means black.

烏 山 Wu-shan, or Oush, the name of a defile in the Aktag mountains, not far from which is the stone tower with forty pillars called *Chihal Situn*, the reputed ruins of a caravan-serai built in Alexander's time.

巫 山 峽 Wu-shan-kiah, one of the most dangerous of the gorges on the Upper Yangtsz'. It is near a mountain of the same name, is 20 miles long, and the boundary between Hupeh and Sech'uen lies about halfway through it. The water of these cliffs or gorges, called *yai-shwui*, is said in the *Pen T'sau* to cause goitre and ague. See Kiu-ying.

烏 什 城 Wu-shih ching, the garrisoned city of Ushi, or Ouchi, in Chinese Turkestan, in the valley of the headwaters of the Tarim river, in Lat. 41° 35′ N. and Long. 77° 50′ E A Chinese officer usually resided here to control the districts of Oksu, Bai and Sairim. By a series of forts he affected to control the wild Kirghis, who have given much trouble to both the Chinese and the Russian generals. This district is separated from I'li and the Kirghis by the *Siueh shan*, on the S. it is bounded by Yarkand and Khoten districts, and E. by that of Aksu.

吳 西 Wu-si, an old name of Kiangsi province.

烏 蘇 里 Wu-su-li, the river Usuri in Kirin.

烏 孫 Wu-sun, a country on the "Western borders," mentioned as producing palms. It was to the king of this country that one of the later Han emperors was made to send one of his daughters.

烏 斯 藏 Wu-sz'-tsang, a name of the Thibetans or Turfans.

五 島 Wu-t'au, the Gotto Islands, off Nagasaki.

五 天 Wu-t'ien, or Goten, the Japanese name of the Getæ, or Massagetæ, or Indo-Scythians, on either side of the Himalayas. See Ta-yueh-chi.

武 都 Wu-tu, an old name of Kiai chau, in Kansuh province.

烏 玉 河 Wu-yuh ho, a river in Khoten yielding jade. See Yuh-lung ho.

兀 刺 海 Wuh-lah-hai, one of the seven *lu* of the Mongolian period, incuding Tangut, or Kansuh. This was probably the kingdom of *Egrigaia* of Marco Polo.

勿 吉 Wuh-kih, the name of the Moh-hoh previous to the Sui dynasty. They were divided into seven tribes, of which Nu-chin and Puh hai were names.

勿 些 Wuh-sié, or Butsa, Bussorah in the Persian Gulf. Remusat gives *Pei-sz'-li* as a name of Bussorah.

Y

雅 克 薩 Ya-keh-sah, Yacsa, the fort of Albazin at the junction of the river Yacsa with the Sagalien ula. It was built by the Russians, and destroyed for the second time, according to treaty in 1689. See Ngo-kwoh-niu-lu.

瓦 剌 Ya-lah, a name of the Mongolian Urats, said to be W. of the Tah-tsu.

雅 魯 藏 布 Ya-lu-tsang-pu, the Yaritsangbo river, variously described in European maps as the Irawaddy or the Brahmaputra river. There is now little doubt that this name properly applies to the Brahmaputra, taking its rise in Western Thibet. The Irawaddy is the *Lu-kiang* of the Chinese. The Ho-ti kiang and Mekong are also important rivers in Yunnan draining neighbouring countries.

亞 細 亞 州 Ya-si-ya chau, the continent of Asia, which with Europe, Lybia (Africa), America and Magellanica, constitutes a dividing of the world in the later Chinese geographies, based upon the manuscripts of the Jesuits. Magellanica included Terra del Fuego, South Shetland, Palmer's Land, &c.

亞 齊 Ya-tsí, Acheen in the N. of Sumatra. See San-fuh-tsí.

楊 州 Yang chau, one of Yü's provinces, including Kiangnan, Kiangsi, Chekiang, Fuhkien, and a small part of Kwangtung.

羊 城 Yang ching, the "City of Rams," a name given to the city of Canton from a legend concerning five shepherds, turned into as many rams, which were again changed into as many stone figures. The five rams in effigy were supposd to be the *palladia* of Canton, and their destruction by fire was superstitiously connected with the decline of the prosperity of the city. It is right to add that some ingeniously refer the name to an accidental resemblance between the characters for *yang* and *yueh*.

陽 穀 縣 Yang-kuh hien, see Tung-ngo hien.

牂 柯 江 Yang-ko kiang, a river in Kwangsi, giving its name to Hwai-yuen hien.

羊 白 頭 Yang-peh-t'u, a name for Albinoes. See Peh-t'u-jin. They are called T'ien-lau-rh, in Peking.

漾 水 Yang shwui, a name of the river Han in the higher part of its course.

楊 子 江 Yang-tsz'-kiang, the river Yangtsz'. See Ta Kiang. This river was sometimes called *Min kiang* in its upper course, from the fact that the Chinese took the *Min* as the largest of the four rivers which drain Sech'uen, and amalgamate to form the Yangtsz'. In the 廣 輿 記, Kwang-yu-ki, there is a story to the effect that a man of I-ching-hien having directed a soldier to fetch some water from the Kiang, was being imposed upon as to the source of the water produced by the man, until his friend upset half of the water, and proved that the remaining half in the bottom of the vessel was alone genuine water of the Kiang. This he proved by splashing the water with a ladle, displaying the characteristic qualities of the water, and was confirmed by the confession of the man that he had added water of another sort. This marvellous fact is supposed to have been commemorated by giving the name 楊 子, Yang-tsz' to the Kiang, 楊, Yang being the character for "splashing." This is however an improbable derivation, for 楊 子, Yang-tsz' was a name of I-ching hien in the time of the T'ang. 江 陽, Kiang-yang was a name of the adjoining district of 江 都, Kiang-tu during the same period.

猺 Yau, a tribe of Miau-tsz' in Li-po hien in Kweichau province. An excellent kind of cassia, produced in their district, is named after them.

夜 郎 Ye-lang, a large country to the S.W. of China, connected with the Laos tribes.

葉 爾 羌 城 Yeh-rh-kiang ching, Yerkiang, or Yarkand, a large city in Chinese Turkestan, on a branch of the river Tarim, in Lat. 38° 19′ N., and Long. 77° 28′ E. See Sha-ku kwoh.

兗 州 Yen chau, one of Yü's nine provinces, including a small part of Pehchihli and of Shantung of the present day.

焉 支 Yen-chi, See Yung-chang-lu and Oh-shi.

焉 耆 Yen-k'i, an old name of Kharashar, said to yield a valuable ophthalmic medicine, called *luh yen*, " green salt, " apparently a kind of malachite, but often adulterated with verditer and verdigris.

燕 京 Yen king, a name of Peking as the seat of a principality in the early Ming period, whose occupant, the fourth son of Hung-wu, seized the throne of his grandnephew and removed the capital from Nanking to Peking, then called Yen king. Yen-shan and Yen kwoh are still older names of what is now Sh-uut'ien fu, the metropolitan prefecture. See Yu-yen and Peh-p'ing. Yen by itself stood for the province of Yu chau, of the Shang dynasty, answering nearly to Pehchihli.

嚴 國 Yen kwoh, a country belonging to Sogdiana, and answering to the modern Yengi kurghan.

嚈 噠 Yen-tah, or Yah-tah, a country of the Massagetæ, in the W. which sent an embassy to China in the reign of Ming Ti of the Western Tsin, in conjunction with the countries T'u-tah and Hwan-tang-chang.

烟 臺 Yen-t'ai, the actual treaty-port in the bay of Chefoo, situated on the northern side of the Shantung promontory, in Lat. 37° 35′ 56″ N., and Long. 121° 22′ 23″ E. This port, miscalled Chefoo, is resorted to as a sanitarium by foreign residents in China, and has the advantage of certain hot springs, called *Tung-t'ang*, at a distance of some fifty miles.

鹽 澤 Yen-tseh, a name of Lake Lop nor. Marco Polo speaks of the city of Lop, which stood in the line of the caravans which here crossed the Great Desert, on their way to China. See Lo-pu-nau-rh.

鹽池 Yen-t'si, a salt lake in Hotung, 160 *li* in circumference.

崦嵫山 Yen-tsz' shan, the name of an imaginary mountain in the W. in which the sun was supposed to rest at night.

益州 Yih chau, an old name of Ching-tu fu, in Sech'uen, under Ts'in.

一賜樂業殷 Yih-tsz'-loh-nieh-tien, the "Temple of the Israelites" at K'aifung fu. The large stone graven with these titular characters has been appropriated by the Mahommedans of that city for their mosque, together with the larger part of the congregation. See K'ai-fung fu.

殷 Yin, the name of the latter part of the Shang dynasty, commencing with P'wan-kang, who shifted the capital from 邢, Hing, in the S.W. of Pehchihli to 亳 Poh in Honan, the old capital of Kuh Kau-sin, the predecessor of T'ang Ti-yau. This was the original capital of the Shang sovereigns.

印度境 Yin-tu-king, the country of India. See T'ien-chuh kwoh, and T'ien-tuh.

印度洋 Yin-tu yang, the Indian Ocean, called in some works the Nan-hai, or Siau-si-yang.

英吉沙爾城 Ying-kih-sha-rh ching, Yingeshar or Yengihassar, a small garrisoned town between the districts of Yarkand and Kashgar, placed W. of Yarkand. See I-nai kwoh.

應天 Ying-t'ien, a name of Nanking under the Ming.

營子 Ying-tsz', or Yun-tsz', the actual port and settlement mis-called Newchwang, situated on the river, at about five miles from its mouth.

岳州 Yoh-chau, or Yoh-chau fu, a town in Hunan, at the mouth of the T'ung-ting lake. It is a military and customs station and is distant from Hankow 130 miles, and from Peking 4,250 *li*. It was the ancient seat of the San miau.

豫章 Yu-chang, an official designation of Kiangsi province. This name, originally given to Nan-chang fu, also called *Hung-tu* was extended to the whole province, as is often the case with the name of the premier *fu* city. This name seems to be sometimes referred to the Kiukiang fu of the present day.

豫州 Yu chau, one of Yü's nine provinces, including six departments in Honan of the present day, two districts in Peh-chih-li, four districts in Shantung, four districts and one sub-department in Nganhwui, and some eight districts or sub-departments in Hupeh. As the greater part of the region lay in Honan, this latter province is sometimes called by this name.

幽州 Yu chau, one of the provinces of Yu-tí-shun, identical with one of a similar name in the Shang dynasty; with the province of Yen (See Yen-king), and the present Pehchihli.

嵎夷 Yu-i, or 東嵎夷, Tung-yu-í, the country of the rising sun referred by some to Corea, and by others to Tang-chau on the Shantung promontory. This depends on the limits assigned to the province of T'sing-chau of Yü's time. The sea has probably encroached here in some way. See Ts'ing chau.

豫寍 Yu-ning, an old name of Wu-ning fu in Kiangsi province.

魚皮達子 Yu-p'i-tah-tsz', the tribe of "Fish-skin Tartars," hunting upon the banks of the Usuri river, in the maritime province of Kirin. These with the *Kiching Tahtsz'* and the *Ghuilaks*, are practically independent of the Chinese government.

于闐國 Yu-tien kwoh, the country of Khoten, the *Casia* of Ptolemy, famous for its silks and jadestone. See Ho-tien.

洫澤 Yu-tseh, a name of the P'u-chang hai   See Lo-pu-nau-rh.

漁陽 Yu-yang, an old name of P'ing-kuh hien (Chihli).

幽薊 Yu-yen, a name of Peking during the Chau dynasty, still used in documents.

粵 Yueh, the old name of the region of Kwangtung, also called *Yueh-tung* to distinguish it from *Yueh-si*, or Kwangsi. 百粵, *Peh yueh* is the old name of a portion of this region.

越 Yueh, an ancient state in the present Chekiang province. See Nan-yueh and Wu.

越裳 Yueh-chang, the Laos tribes between Yunnan and Annam and Siam.

粵匪 Yueh-fei, the name by which the *Ch'ang-mau*, or rebel followers of the *T'ai-ping wang*, from Kwangsi and Kwangtung, are spoken of in official documents.

越南 Yueh-nan, or Annam, Cochin China, called by the Cochin Chinese *Vietnam*. Kwang-tung or Canton province was formerly called *Nan-yueh*, to distinguish it from the *Yueh kwoh* of Chekiang. *Tung-yueh* is an old name of *Shau-hing fu* in Chekiang, famous for its silk.

越析詔 Yueh-sih-cháu, a name of one of the six chiefs of the tribes of the province of Yunnan, called *Caraian* by Marco Polo. This province was then inhabited by those tribes, probably to be identified with the Karens, who had been conquered by the Mongols. See Ngai-lau-í.

月氏 Yueh-ti, the Getæ or Indo-Scythians, conquerors of Scinde and the Punjaub, about the early part of the Christian era. See Ta-yuch-chi, and Mih-kieh kwoh.

元 Yuen, the Mongolian race and dynasty. See Mung-ku.

員渠城 Yuen-ku ching, Yengu, a town near Kharashar formerly the capital of the district.

元兔 Yuen-t'u, an ancient kingdom in Liautung, afterwards made into a principality by Wu Ti of the Han dynasty.

郁 Yuh, the name of an ancient region in the S.E. of Kansuh and adjoining part of Shensi of the present time. There was a *Yuh-chih hien* in Shantung.

郁郅 Yuh-chih, an ancient name of *Ngan-hwa hien* in Kansuh.

玉籠河 Yuh-lung ho, the Yurung Kash, or Ulgunkash, a river near Ilchi in Chinese Tur-kestan, whose swollen streams bring down nephrite or jade, which is collected from the bed or strand. This is the Khoten river of some writers. See Keh-lah-keh-sha.

玉門關 Yuh-mon-kwan, a barrier or pass in the W. in Chinese Turkestan.

營州 Yun chau, a name given to Liautung by Shun, who separated it from Yü's province of Ts'ing chau.

雲中 Yun chung, a region in the ancient K'i-chau province, answering to the present depart-ment of *Ta-t'ung-fu* in Shansi, still bearing this alias. It was the early capital of the Wei kingdom.

雲漢 Yun-han, or the Milky Way. See T'ien ho.

運河 Yun-ho, or Yun-liang ho, the "Grain-transporting river," the Grand Canal.

運 糧 河 Yun-liang ho, or Yun ho, the Grand Canal. See Chah ho.

管 子 Yun-tsz', see Ying-tsz. This name scarcely means "the camp," as it is translated in some foreign works, for the pronunciation is quite distinct. The name is probably derived from the name of the old province of *Yun chau*, separated by Shun from Ts'ing chau when he extended Yü's pet number of nine provinces to twelve in all.

永 昌 路 Yung-chang lu, one of the Mongolian divisions of China, answering to the *tau* of the T'ang period. This is now the head of a district in Kansuh, in Lat. 38° 20′ N. and Long. 101° E. It was the city of *Erguiul* of Marco Polo. This district was formerly called *Yen-chi*.

雝 州 Yung chau, the largest of Yü's provinces, to the N. of Liang chau, and separated from K'i chau by the *Si ho*, which see.

榕 城 Yung ching, the "Banian city," a name of Fuhchau.

永 寕 城 Yung-ning ching, the "City of eternal tranquillity," a name given to Ushi by K'ien-lung, after the conquest of Turkestan.

Z

INDEX.

A

Abagais. See A-pa-kai.

Abaganar. See A-pa-ha-nah-rb.

Aborigines. See Miau-tsz'. Nui-i. Nung-jin.
San-miau. Siau-kin-ch'uen. Tan. Tau-kia.
Yau. Pei-lau.

Achaia. See Wu-c'hi-kwoh.

Acheen. See Ya-tsi.

Adam. See A-tan.

Adam's peak. See Sih-lan-shan.

Afghanistan. See Ki-pin-kwoh.

Africa. See Li-wei-ya.

Aimaks. See Choh-lo-sz'-pu.

Ainos. See Hia-i.

Aksai-chin. See Lo-to-keh ching.

Aksu. See A-keh-su ching. Wan-suh.

Albasins. See Ngo-kwoh-niu-luh. Ya-keh-sah.

Albinoes. See Peh-min-kwoh. Yang-peh-t'u.

Alotan river. See A-keh-tan-ho.

Alps. See Siau-kwan-lun.

Altai mountains. See Kin-shan.

Altchucu. See A-leh-keh-tsu ching.

Amarapura. See P'u-kan.

Amazons. See Nu-tsz'-kwoh.

Amban. See Ko-pu-to-ching.

Amboyna. See Ngan-wan.

America. See Hwa-k'i-kwoh. Mei-kwoh.

Amoy. See Hia-men. Hai-t'au. Lu-kiang.

Amur river. See Heh-lung-kiang.

Annam. See Cochinchina.

Antoninus. See An-tan.

Arabia. See Ta-shih-kwoh. T'ien-fang kwoh.
T'ien-t'ang.

Aria. See Hai-ya-kwoh.

Arzobispo islands. See Wu-jin-t'au.

Asia. See Ya-si-ya-chau.

Atlantic ocean. See Ta-si-yang-hai.

Austria. See Tsz'-ying. Tuh-yih.

Áykhom. See Ngai-hwan-ching.

Azure sea. See T'sing-hai.

B

Bactria. See Ta-hia.

Badakshan. See Pa-teh-keh-shan.

Bai. See Pai-ching.

Balkh. See Ta-hia.

Banca. See San-lih.

Banchin-erdeni. See Chah-shih-lun-pu-ching.

Banjermassing. See Ma-shin.

Bantam. See Tan-tan-kwoh. Wan-tan. Tu-po-
kwoh.

Barbarians. See Hien-yun. I'. Jung-tih. Man.
Moh-yau. Shan-jung. Si-hu. Si-kiang.
Sien-li. Su-jung. Tih. Wai-fan. Wai-i.
Hung-i. Peh-lan.

Barin. See Pa-lin.

Barkul. See Chin-si. Pa-rh-ku-rh.

Bashee islands. See Hung-t'u-sû.

Batavia. See Kia-liu-pa. Koh-lah-pa.

Bathang. See Pa-t'ang.

Bayenkara. See Pa-yen-k'eh-lah.

Behar. See Mo-kieh-t'i-kwoh.

Belur tagh. See T'sung-ling.

Benares. See Po-lo-nai.

Bencoulen. See Wan-ku-lu. Wang-kiu-li.

Bengal. See P'ang-koh-lah.

Bich balish. See Peh-ting.

Bima. See Li-ma.

Bisch balik. See Ho-chau.

Black-tented Thibetans. See Si-fan.

Black Tartars. See Hiau-lo-ko-muh-li.

Bokhara. See A-pa-ko-rh. Fan-tu-ching.

Bombay. See Tan kwoh.

Bonin islands. See Wu-jin-t'au.

Bonzes. See Fan-sang.

Borneo. See Fuh-ni. Po-lo-chau. P'o-ni. Puh-ni.
Wan-lai. Liu-kiu kwoh. P'o-luh kwoh.

Botel Tobago. See Hung-t'u-sû.

Bourouts. See Pu-lu-teh.

Brahma. See Fan.

Brahmaputra river. See Ta-kin-sha-kiang. Ya-

In-tsang-pu.

Brahmins. See Fan. Po-lo-men.

British legation. See Liang-kung-fu.

Budala. See Pu-tah-la.

Buddha. See A-mi-to-fuh. F'an-t'ú. Ju-lai-fuh. Mi-leh-fuh. Nan-wu a-mi-to-fuh. Shih-kia-man-ni.

Buddhism. See Fuh-kiau. Shih-kiau.

Buddhist priests. See Fan-sang. Fan-t'ú. Sang-men. Sha-men.

Burmah. See A-wa. Mien-tien. Chú-po-ti.

Burmans. See Po-lo-men.

Bussorah. See Wu-sié.

Byzantium. See Fuh-lin-kwoh.

C

Cabul. See Ngan-shih-kwoh. Pu-lu-sha-pu-lo. T'u-lin.

Cacian fu. See Ho-chung-fu.

Calatia. See Chung-hing-fu Ning-hia.

Calicut. See Ku-li. Si-yang-ku-li.

California. See Kin-shan.

Cambodia. See Chin-lah. Fu-nan. Nan-man-kwoh. Tung-p'u-chai.

Camoens's grotto. See Peh-koh-c'hau.

Cancun. See Han-chung. Hing-yuen-lu.

Candahar. See Kia-t'u-lo.

Canfu. See Cha-pu. Kan-p'u.

Cangigu. See Pap-peh-sih-fuh kwoh.

Canton city. See Kwang-chau-fu. Yang-ching.

Canton province. See Ling-nan. Nan-yueh. Tung-yueh. Yueh.

Capital of Annam. See Kiau-chau-fu.

Capital of Burmah. See A-wa. P'ang-hiang. P'u-kan. Ta-kang kwoh.

Capitals of China. See Hien-yang. Chang-ngan. Loh-yang. Ching-tu-lu. Ngoh-chü. Kien-yeh. Si-ngan-fu. Puh-chau. Pien-chau. Peh-king. Yen-king. Nan-king.

Capital of Corea. See King-ki-tau.

Caraian. See Kau-ting. Luh-chán. Yueh-sih-chán.

Caramoran. See Hwang-ho.

Garlmon islands. See Kih-li-men.

Casa Branca. See T'sien-shan-chai.

Cashmere. See Kia-shih-mi-lo.

Caspian sea. See Lui-hai. Si-hai.

Cathay. See K'i-tan.

Celebes islands. See Si-li-chih.

Celestials. Mung-ku-jin.

Celestial mountains. See T'ien-shan.

Central India. See Chung-t'ien-chuh.

Ceram. See Si-lan.

Ceylon. See Sih-lan-shan-kwoh. Sz'-tsz'-kwoh.

Chamdo. See Tsiando.

C'hang-mau. See T'ai-pings.

Chapu. See Chá-pu.

Chefoo. See Chi-fau. Tang-chau-fu. Yen-t'ai.

Chersonesus. See Wan-lai.

Chihal Situn. See Wu-shan.

Chluchew. See T'siuen-chau fu.

China. See Chi-na. Chin-tan. C'hih-ni. Chu-hia. Chung-kwoh. Chung-hwa. Han-t'u. Hwa-hia. Shih-pah-sang. Ta-t'sing-kwoh. T'ang-shan. Tung-t'u. T'ien-chau.

China sea. See Tung-hai.

Chinese emigrants. See T'ang-jin.

Chiangmai. See Chau-mei.

Chonka. See Kien-kwoh.

Choros tribes. See Choh-lo-sz'-pu.

Choshots. See Choh-soh-t'u-ming.

Chusan. See Chau-shan.

Ciandu. See Shang-tu.

Clemeinfu. See K'ai-p'ing.

Cochin. See Kwei-tsing.

Cobdo. See Ko-pu-to-ching.

Cochinchina. See Chiau-chi. Hwang-chi-kwoh. Jeh-nan. Kiu-chin. Nan-chiau-chi-ti. Ngan-nan-kwoh. Si-king.

Cogacin. See Ho-keh-tsi.

Cophené. See Ki-pin-kwoh.

Coromandel coast. See A-c'hih-li-kwoh. Kau-shih-tah.

Corea. See Chau-sien. Kau-li-kwoh.

Cossacks. See Ha-sah-keh.

Coulan. See Kú-lan.

Cush. See Hindoo Kush.

Cretins. See Kiu-ying. Wu-shan-kiah.

Cyamba. See Tsiampa.

D

Dahro. See Ta-hia.

Dainam. See T'ai-nan. Ta-yueh.

Dalai Lama. See Tah-lai-lah-ma. Chah-shih-lun-pu-ching.

Diourian mountains. See Ken-teh-shan.

Deccan. See Ta-king.

Denmark. See Hwang-k'i-kwoh.

Desert of Gobi. See Han-hai. Ko-pih. Liu-sha. Sha-moh.

Desima. See Chuh-t'au.

Dharma. See Ta-fah-kwoh.

Djassi. See Chah-shih-ching.
Doloudo. Lah-ma-miau.
Dsiloung. See Tsi-lung-ching.
Dsunggar. See Tsung-keh-ching.
Durbeths. See Tu-rh-peh-teh.
Dutch. See Ho-lan-kwoh. Hung-man. Chuh-t'au.
Dyaks. See Li-mau-jau.

E

East India Company. See Kung-sz'.
Egrigaia. See Ning-hia. Wuh-lah-hai.
Egypt. See Mi-sz'-rh.
Eight pasturages. See Pah-yuen.
Eleuths. See A-lu-shan ngeh-lu-teh-k'i. Ngeh-lu-teh. Ha-mih.
Emperor of China. See T'ien-tsz'. T'ien-chau.
England. See Ta-ying-kwoh.
Erguiul. See Yung-chang-lu.
Europe. See Ngau-lo-pa. Si-yang. Ta-si-yang.

F

Fahan. See Ku-san-kwoh.
Fan-ching. See Siang-ho.
Fan tribes. See Chang-ye. Chu-fan. Mung-fan. Si-fan. Wai-fan.
Fatshan. See Fuh-shan.
Feiyaks. See Fei-ya-keh.
Ferganah. See Ta-yuen-kwoh.
Firando. See Ping-hu-t'au.
Fischer's island. See P'ang-hu.
Fish-skin Tartars. See Yu-p'i-tah-tsz'.
Fohi. See P'au-hi.
Foreign-office. See Li-fan-yuen. T'sung-li-ya-men.
Formosa. See P'i-shié-ye. T'ai-wan.
Fort Vernöe. See Kashgar.
France. See Ta-fah-kwoh. Fuh-lang-si.
Franks. See Fuh-lang-ki.
French. See Fuh-lang-ki. Fu-lang-si.
Fuchow. See Fuh-chau. Sau-shan. Yung-ching.
Fukien. See Kien-kwoh. Min.
Fusiyama. See Fu-sz'-shan.
Fyzabad. See Pa-tah-keh-shan.

G

Ganga river. See Kang-hoh.
Ganges. See Hang-ho. King-kia.
Gautama Buddha. See Shih-kia-mau-ni.
Genghis Khan. See Ching-kih-sz'-han.

Getæ. See Ta-yueh-chi. Wu-t'ien. Yueh-ti.
Ghieding. See Kieh-ting ching.
Ghioro. See Koh-lo.
Ghoorkas. See Koh-rh-k'eh.
Girin. See Kirin.
Goa. See Siau-si-yang.
Gobi desert. See Han-hai. Ko-pih. She-moh.
Gotto islands. See Wu-t'au.
Grand Canal. See Chah-ho. Yun-liang-ho.
Great Britain. See Ta-ying-kwoh.
Great Wall. See Shan-hai-kwan. Si-ho-chau. Tsz'-seh. Wan-li-chang-ching.
Greeks. See Hi-li-ni. Wu-c'hi-kwoh.
Gugé. See Ku-keh.
Guldscha. See Hwui-yuen-ching.
Gunga. See Hang-ho. Kang-hoh.
Gutzlaff island. See Ma-tsih.

H

Hai-men. See Tsung-ming-hien.
Hainan. See Hai-k'au. Kiung-chau. Pei-lau.
Hakkas. See Keh-kia. Pun-ti.
Hakodadi. See Shiang-kwan.
Hakusai. See Poh-tsi.
Hamil. See Ha-mih. I-wu-lu.
Hangchow. See King-sz'. Lin-ngan. Wu-'in. Hai-t'ang.
Hankow. See Han-k'au. Siang-ho.
Hankow settlement. See Shih-pah-sang.
Hanlemuh. See Sai-li-muh-ching.
Hanyang. See Ngoh-chü. T'sing-ch'uen. Tnn-yang. Han-tsin, and Han-yang-kwan.
Hanyang hill. See Ta-pieh-shan.
Haröyu. See Herat.
Hassacks. See Ha-sah-keh.
Hebrew. See Hi-peh-lai.
Herat. See Hai-ya-kwoh.
Himalayas. See Sineh-shan.
Himatala. See Sineh-shan-hia.
Hindoo Kush. See Hien-tu.
Hindostan. See Han-tu-sz'-tan. Wan-tu-sz'-tan.
Il'lari. See La-li-ching.
Il'lassa. See La-sah. Pu-tah-la.
Hreifan hotun. See Hwui-fah.
Hoklo. See Fuh-lau.
Holland. See Ho-lan-kwoh. Hung-man.
Honan. See Chung-yuen. Yu-chau.
Hongque. See Hung-k'au.
Hongkong. See Hiang-kiang. K'wan-tai-lu.
Horiads. See Urats.
Hormaz. See Ku-li-kwoh and Hwuh-lu-mu-sz'.

Hoshoits. See Ho-shih-teh-pu.

Hot springs. See K'eh-lah-k'eh-sha. Yen-t'ai.
Jeh-ho.

Hotun tala. See Ngoh-tun-ta-la. Sing-suh-hai.

Hué. See Kiau-chau-fu.

Hunan. See Hu-kwang. San-siang. Siang-
chung.

Hung-tu. See Yu-chang.

Hupeh. See Tiung-ting-hu. San-t'sú.

Hurha river. See Ning-ku-tah-ching. San-sing-
ching.

Hurun-pir. See Hu-lun-pei-rh-ching.

Hwan-wang. See Lin-yih.

I

I-bo-bien. See Pa-rh-ku-rh.

Ilchí. See Ho-tien-ching.

I'li. See Hwui-yuen-ching.

India. See Chau-sien-t'ien-tuh. Chung-t'ien-
chuh. Kiuen-tuh. Shin-tuh. Si-t'ien. T'ien-
chuh-kwoh. T'ien-tuh. Yin-tu-king.

Indian Ocean. See Nan-hai. Yin-tu-yang.

Indo-scythians. See Ta-yueh-chí. Wu-t'ien.
Yueh-tí.

Indus. See Kang-hoa. Ma-peh-moh-tah-lai.
Shin-tuh.

Inner Mongolia. See Mung-ku.

Irawaddy river. See Lu-kiang. Nu-kiang. Ya-
lu-tsang-pu.

Islam. See Sih-t'í.

Italy. See I'-ta-li-ya.

J

Jambi. See Kü-kiang.

Japan. See Hwang-kwoh. Jeh-pun. Jeh-pun-
kwoh. Shin-kwoh. Tung-yang. Wei-kwoh.

Japanese. See Wei-nu. Wei-tsz'.

Japan sea. See Siau-tung-yang.

Jau-jen. See Ju-ju.

Java. See Chau-wa. Kia-liu-pa. Koh-lah-pa.

Javanese. See Chau-ya.

Jaya. See Cha-ya.

Jehol. See Jeh-ho. Pi-shu-shan-chwang.

Jen-fci. See Ju-jn.

Jesus. See Rh-sa.

Jews. See Kiu-kiau. Lan-mau-hwui-tsz'. Mwan-
lah. Tau-kin-kiau. T'ien-chuh-kiau. T'ien-
kiau. T'sing-chin-kiau. Yih-tsz'-loh-nieh-tien.

Jiling, or Siling. See Si-ning.

Johore. See Jau-fuh.

Jounghia. See Jung-hiah-ching.

Judæa. See Ju-teh-ya. Fuh-lin-kwoh.

Junk-seylon. See Sih-lan.

Jupiter. See Sheh-t'i.

Juts. See Ta-yueh-chi.

K

Kalantan. See Kia-lan-tan.

Kalgan. See Chang-kia-k'au. Mai-mai-chin.

Kalkas. See K'eh-rh-k'eh.

Kambalu. See Peh-king.

Kanagawa. See Shin-nai-ch'uen.

Kansuh. See Wan-t'siuen. Peh-ti-kiun.

Kara Kitai. See Hiau-lo-ko-muh-li. K'i-tan.

Karakorum. See Ho-lin. Ho-ning.

Karakash. See K'eh-lah-k'eh-sha.

Karens. See Kau-ting. Luh-cháu. Ngai-lau-i.
Wu-man.

Kartsin. See K'eh-lah-tsin.

Kashgar. See K'eh-shih-kieh-rh-ching. Su-leh-
kwoh.

Kekichten. See Keh-si-keh-tang.

Kelung. See Ki-lung. Shié-liau.

Kentei mountains. See Ken-teh-shan.

Kerman. See Tu-po-lo-men.

Kewkiang. See Kiu-kiang.

Kham. See Kang. Chah-muh-to-ching.

Khamba. See Kang. Keh-muh.

Khaotchit. See Kau-tsi-teh.

Kharachin. See K'eh-lah-tsin.

Kharashar. See K'eh-lah-sha-rh-ching. Yen-k'i.

Khoits. See Hwui-teh-pu.

Khojend. See Hoh-su.

Khorlos. See Koh-lo-rh-sz'.

Khoten. See Ho-tien-ching. Yu-tien-kwoh.

Khoten river. See Wu-yuh-ho. Ho-tien-ching.
Yuh-lung-ho.

Khoubdam. See Chang-ngan.

Kiachta. See Mai-mai-chin.

Kibi. See Kih-pi.

Ki-hu-wan. See Kublai Khan.

K'ih-lau. See Lau-tsz'.

Kin Tartars. See Nu-chih. Ta-kin.

Kr'afto. See Peh-hia-i.

Kinsai. See King-sz'.

Kioto. See King-tu.

Kirghis. See Ha-sah-keh. Wu-shih-ching.

Kirin. See Kih-lin.

Kokand. See Hoh-han. Ta-yuen-kwoh.

Kokonor. See Ku-ko-noh-rh. T'sing-hai.

Kolo tribes. See Si-fan.

Ko-lo-fu-sha. See Ta-ni.

Koran. See Ku-leh.

Korchins. See A-lu-ko-rh-tsin.

Kortchins. See Ko-rh-tsin.

Koûbo. See Hung-fah.

Koulkun mountains. See Kwan-lun. Nan shan. Siau-kwan-lun.

Koutché. See Ku-ché-ching. Kwei-tsz'-kwoh.

Kowloong. See Kiu-lung.

Koxinga. See Ching-chi-lung. Kwoh-sing-ye. Tung-ning.

Ku-yeh-t'au. See Peh-hia-í.

Kublai Khan. See Hwuh-pieh-lieh.

Kukai Mongol. See Mung-ku-jin.

Kuku kotu. See Kwei-shu-ching.

Kukuktu. See Ku-lun.

Kuldja. See Guldscha.

Kung. See Prince Kung.

Kurkara usu. See Ku-rh-k'eh-lah wu-su-ching.

Kurun. See Ku-lun.

Kwan-yin. See Mi-leh-fuh. Nan-hai. Kwan-shi-yin.

L

Ladak. See La-tah-keh.

Ladrone islands. See Lau-wan-shan.

Lake Baikal. See Peh-hai.

Lake Barkul. See Hiung-nu-chung-hai. P'u-lu-hai.

Lampong. See Lan-fang.

Langya-nor. See Ma-peh-moh-tah-la.

Lanka. See Ceylon.

Larin. See La-lin-ching.

Latin. See Li-han.

Leh. See La-tah-keh.

Leulan. See Shen-shen.

Lewchew islands. See Chung-shan. Liu-kiu-kwoh. Na-pa. Shau-ni.

Liampo. See Ning-po-fu.

Libya. See Li-wei-ya.

Linga. See Lang-ya.

Lintin island. See Ling-t!ng.

Lithang. See Li-t'ang.

Lohyang. See I'-kien.

Lolo. See Sien-lo. Luh-lai.

Lop-nor. See Lo-pu-nan-rh. P'u-chang-hai. Yen-tseh. Yu-tseh.

Lucon. See Lu-sung.

Lu-men, or Lu-t'au. See Hia-men and Hia-t'au.

Lunar race. See Ta-yueh-chí.

M

M'abar. See Ma-pah-rh.

Macao. See Ngau-men.

Macao barrier. See Kwan-chah.

Macao roads. See Sha-lih.

Macassar. See Mang-kia-sah.

Madjicosima islands. See Kung-ku-tau.

Madura. See Mo-tu-lo.

Magadha. See Fan. Mo-kia-to-kwoh. Mo-kieh-t'i-kwoh. P'o-so-kwoh.

Magellanica. See Ya-si-ya-chau.

Mahommed. See Moh-han-meh-teh.

Mahommedans. See Hwui-hwui. Kiau-men. Moh-min. Sih-ti. Si-mi-kwoh-wang. Tu-wan-siu.

Mahommedan tribes. See Fu-lu-rh. Hwui-pu.

Maitreya. See Mi-leh-fuh.

Malabar. See Ku-li-kwoh.

Malacca. See Ma-luh-kiah. Man-luh-kia.

Malaysia. See Kia-lan-tan. Ta-ni. Sien-lo. Jau-fuh.

Manchuria. See Mwan-chau.

Manchus. See Koh-lo. Mwan-jin. Nu-chih. T'sing. Moh-hoh. Wuh-kih.

Manicheans. See Moh-ni.

Manilla. See Kwei-tau. Lu-sung. Siau-lu-sung.

Manji. See Man. Man-tsz'.

Mao mingan. See Mau-min-ngan.

Marco Polo. See Chû-mih-fuh-sz'. Poh-lo.

Marcus Aurelius Antoninus. See An-tan.

Mar-yul. See La-tah-keh.

Massagetæ. See Mih-kieh-kwoh. Ta-yueh-chi. Wo-t'ien. Yen-tah. Yueh-ti.

Masulipatam. See Ku-li-pan-tsuh.

Mattoo Ricci. See Li-ma-tuh.

Mecca. See Meh-keh-kwoh. Moh-kia.

Medina. See Meh-teh-na.

Mediterranean sea. See Si-hai. Ta-hai. Ti-chung-hai.

Meiacosima. See Madjicosima. Kung-ku-t'au.

Meikong river. See Kiu-lung-kiang. Nan-chang-kiang.

Merguen. See Meh-rh-kan-ching.

Miaco. See King-tu.

Middle Kingdom. See Chung-chau. Chung-kwoh.

Mikado. See T'ien-tsz'. Kung-fang.

Milky way. See T'ien-ho. Yun-han.

Mindoro. See T'au-ho.

Moh-hu. See Moh-min.

Moluccas. See Mi-luh-hoh. Mei-loh-ku. Si-lan.

Mongolia. See Mung-ku.

Mongols. See A-pa-ha-nah-rh. Chah-lai-teh. Chah-lu-teh. Chah-wn-tah ming. Chi-li-muh ming. Choh-soh-t'u ming. I-keh-chau ming. K'eh-lah-tsin. Koh-rh-lo-sz'. Mung-ku-jin. Nai-man. Ngau-han. Sih-lin-koh-lih ming. Tu-rh-hu-teh-pu.

Moors. See Peh-t'u-jin.

Moses. See Mo-sa.

Moukden. See Shing-king-pun-ching. Fung-t'ien-fu.

Moulmein. See Tang-yneh-chau.

Mullah. See Mwan-lah.

N

Nagasaki. See Chang-k'i.

Nanking. See Kiang-nan. Kiang-ning. Kien-yeh. Kin-ling. Moh-ling. Nan-ki.

Nari. See A-li-ching. Ku-keh.

Nepaul. See Ni-p'o-lo.

Nestorians. See Ju-li-ya. King-kiau. T'ien-chuh-kiau.

Nestorian tablet. See Si-ngan-fu.

Newchwang. See Niu-chwang. Ying-tsz'.

Nielam. See Nieh-la-pun-ching.

Ningpo. See Ning-po-fu. Sz'-ming. Ming-chau fu.

Ningunta. See Ning-ku-tah-ching.

Nipchú. See Ni-pú-tsú.

Nippon. See Jeh-pun.

North Laos. See Chau-mei. Pah-peh-sih-fuh-kwoh.

Norway. See Shwui-kwoh.

O

Oden. See Ngoh-tang.

Oksu. See A-keh-su-ching. Wan-suh.

Onion mountains. See T'sung-ling.

Onrust. See U-ching.

Oonam. See Hu-nan, under T'ung-ting-hu.

Oopack. See Hu-peh, under T'ung-ting-hu.

Oranbaligh. See Ho-ning.

Orats. See Wu-lah-tih.

Orders of Knighthood. See Pa-t'u-lu. Tieh-mau-tsz'-wang.

Orissa. See Wu-c'ha-kwoh.

Ormus. See Ku-li kwoh.

Ortous. See Ngoh-rh-to-sz'.

Osaka. See Ta-pan.

Ouchi. See Wu-shih-ching.

Oudjumuchins. See Wu-chu-moh-t'sin.

Ouigour. See Uigur.

Ouniots. See Ung-niu-teh.

Ouroumtsi. See Urumtsi.

Oush. See Wu-shan.

Oushi. See Ouchi.

Outer Mongolia. See Mung-ku.

P

Pacific ocean. See Shin-hai. Ta-ming-hai. Ta-hai. T'ai-p'ing-yang. Tung-yang. Wan-shwui-chau-tung-ta-hai. Wei-lu.

Padang. See Pa-tung.

Paghan. See P'ang-hiang.

Paken. See P'ing-t'siuen-chau.

Palaces. See A-ching. Pi-shú-shan-chwang. Siuen-hwa-fu. Tsz'-kin-ching.

Palembang. See Kú-kiang.

Palestine. See Fuh-lin-kwoh. Ju-teh-ya.

Pali language. See Fan. Mo-kieh-t'i-kwoh.

Palisade. See Muh-t'u-ching.

Palm island. See Shié-liau.

Papua. See Pau-pau.

Paracel reefs. See T'sih-chau.

Parsees. See Ho-shin-kiau. Peh-t'u-jin. Po-sz'-king-kiau. Shih-ho-chi-kwoh.

Parthians. See Ngan-sih.

Passir. See Pa-shih.

Patan, or Pattan. See Pà-tàn.

Patani. See Ta-ni.

Pechele. See Peh-chih-li.

Pegassim. See P'ang-hiang.

Pegu. See Peh-ngo. P'i-kien.

Peh-yueh. See Yueh.

Peking. See Peh-king. King-sz'. Shun-t'ien-fu. Ta-tu. Yen-king. Yu-yen.

Penal settlements. See Heh-lung-kiang-ching. Wu-lu-moh-tsi. Hi-chun-ching.

Penang. See Pin-lang. Sin-fau.

Persia. See Po-sz'-kwoh.

Persians. See Hwui-hwui. Hung-mau-hwui-tsz'. Po-sz'-kwoh. Ta-shih.

Pescadore islands. See P'ang-hu.

Peshawur. See Pu-lu-sha-pu-lo.

Petunó ula. See Peh-tu-nah-ching.

Philippine islands. See Manilla.

Philistia. See Fuh-lin kwoh.

Pidjan. See Pih-chen. Shen-shen.

Podzung. See Poh-tsung-ching.

Pontiana. See P'o-ni.

Poonah. See Po-na.

Portugal. See Poh-rh-tu-koh-rh-ya-kwoh. Si-

yang kwoh. Ta-si-yang.
Portuguese. See Fuh-lang-ki. Sih-tsz'-nien.
Postmaster General. See King-t'ang.
Potteries. See King-teh-chin.
Pou-ho-rh. See A-pa-ko-rh.
Poutai ula. See Ta-sang-wu-la-ching.
Poyang lake. See P'ang-li. Poh-yang-hu.
Praya grande. See Nan-wan.
Prince Kung. See Ho-shih-kung-t'sin-wang.
Prussia. See Po-lo-sz'. Tan-ying.
Pulo Condor. See Kwan-t'un.
Pulo Nias. See Ni-shi.
Putek. See Pu-teh-ha-ching.

Q

Quedah. See Kih-tsah.
Quemoy island. See Kin-mun.
Quilon. See Kŭ-lan.

R

Rajagriha. See P'in-p'o-so-lo. Wang-shié.
Rama. See Lan-mo.
Rebels. See T'ien-kwoh. Yueh-fei.
Red Sea. See Hung-hai.
Rodok. See Lo-to-keh-ching.
Roman Catholicism. See T'ien-chŭ-kiau.
Roman empire. See Fuh-lin-kwoh. Hai-si-kwoh.
  Li-han. Ta-t'sin. Wu-c'hi-kwoh.
Russia. See Lu-si-ya. Ngo-kwoh. Ngo-lo-si.
  Ngoh-lo-si.
Russian Mission, Peking. See Ngo-kwoh-niu
  kwoh.

S

Sacai. See Kiu-seh.
Sagalien island. See P'eh-hia-í.
Sagalien river. See Heh-lung-kiang. Kwan-t'ung.
  Sung-hwa-ho.
Sagalien ula. See Heh-lung-kiang-ching.
Saigon. See Chen-ching.
Sairim. See Sai-li-muh-ching.
Salat. See Sih-lah.
Samarang. See San-pau-lung.
Samarcand. See Sah-ma-rh-han. Shié-mi-sz'-han.
Samyó. See Sang-li.
Sancian island. See Shang-ch'uen-shan.
Sangkoi river. Sek Ho-ti kiang.
Sanlak. See Banca.
Sansang. See San-sing-ching.
Sanscrit. See Fan.
Sararchi. See Sah-la-tsí.

Sardansu. See Ching-tu-lu.
Scinde. See Shin-tuh. T'ien-tuh.
Scythians. See Hien-yun. Mih-kieh-kwoh. Ta-
  yueh-chí.
Sechuen. See Ching-tu-lu. Pa-shuh. Shuh.
Secret societies. See Ko-lau. San-hoh-hwui.
Seranis. See Sih-tsz'-nien.
Serfs. See Shen-hu.
Shakyamuni. See Shih-kia-mau-ni.
Shan-yu. See Tan-yu.
Shanghai. See Shang-hai. Hu-tuh.
Shang-kuh. See Siuen-hwa-fu.
Shansi. See Ho-peh. Ho-tung. Si-lu. Tsin-ti.
Shantung. See Tung-lu. Tung-miau.
Shensi. See A-kwan. Kwan-chung. Kwan-lui.
  Shen-chau. T'sin-king.
Sheudi. See Shau-ni.
Shiites. See Ta-shih.
Shobando. See Shih-pan-to-ching.
Shoghnan. See Kang-kŭ.
Siam. See Sien-lo.
Siang-ho-k'au, or Siang-k'au. See Han-k'au.
Siang-yang fu. See Siang-ho.
Siberia. See Hi-kwoh. Sz'-me-li.
Sikok. See Sin-lo.
Silver island. See Tsiáu-shan.
Sindufu. See Ching-tu-lu.
Singanfu. See A-ching. Chang-ngan. Chau-fu.
  Hien-yang. King-chau. Ngan-si. Si-king.
Singapore. See Sih-lah. Sin-kia-po.
Singuy. See Si-ngan-fu.
Sinhala. See Sz'-tsz'-kwoh.
Sinus magnus. See Ta-hai.
Siueh-ling. See Pa-yen-k'eh-lah.
Suake island. See Shié-su.
Sogdiana. See Kang-kŭ.
Sogomornbarkan. See Shih-kia-mau-ni.
Songares. See Ngeh-lu-teh. Ha-mih. Tu-rh-
  hu-teh-pu.
Songari river. See Sung-hwa-ho.
Songaria. See T'ien-shan-peh-lu.
Soochow. See P'ang-ching. San-wu. Wu-chung.
Sora Mikado. See T'ien-tsz'.
Soungar. See Chun-kieh-rh.
Sourabaya. See Sz'-li-mau.
South Laos. See Nan-chang.
Spain. See Shih-pan-niu. Ta-lu-sung.
Sribodja. See Shih-li-fuh-chih.
St. John's island. See Shang-ch'uen-shan.
Suiyip. See Sui-yeh.
Suloo territory. See Su-luh.

Sumatra. See San-fuh-tsi. Su-men-tah-lah.

Sunnites. See Su-ni-teh. Ta-shih. To-lun-noh-rh.

Surat. See Su-ho-t'u.

Su-wan-tah-lah. See Su-mun-tah-lah.

Swatow. See Shan-t'n.

Sweden. See Shwui-kwoh.

Sypangu. See Jeh-pun-kwoh.

Syria. See Ju-li-ya. Ju-teh-ya. T'ien-chuh-kwoh.

T

Tagaung. See Ta-kang-kwoh.

Taipings. See T'ien-kwoh. Yueh-fei.

Taitun. See T'siuen-chau-fu. Hia-t'au.

Tajiks. See Hwui-hwui. Ta-shih. Tu-po-lo-men

Tamerlane. See Tieh-muh-er.

Tamlook. See Tan-mei.

Tamsui. See Tan-sui.

Tanduc. See Ta-t'ung. Yun-chung.

Tang-chang. See Tang-chau.

Tangut. See Ho-si. Kau-chang. Tang-hiang. T'sing-hai.

Taprobane. See Tu-po-kwoh.

Tarakai. See Peh-hia-i. T'au-i.

Tarbagatai. See Tah-rh-pa-ha-tai-ching.

Tarim river. See Lo-pu-nau-rh. P'u-chang-hai.

Tartar princes. See Kung-t'sin-wang

Tartars. See K'i. Pah-k'i. Ta-kin. Tah-tah-rh. Yu-p'i-tah-tsz'.

Tashtava. See Tarbagatai.

Tasigan. See Tah-shih-kan.

Tatars. See Tah-tan. Mung-ku-jin.

Tathagata. See Ju-lai-fuh.

Temugin. See Ching-kih-sz'-kan. Teh-moh-chin

Tenasserim. See Tun-sun.

Tengri tagh. See Tang-keh-li. T'ien-shan.

Teshu-h'lumbu. See Chah-shih-lun-pu-ching. Jeh-hoh-tseh.

Teshu-lama. See Chah-shih-lun-pu-ching.

Thibet. See Hau-tsang. Si-tsang. T'sien-tsang. T'u-peh-teh. Wei-tsang. Wu-sz'-tsang.

Thibetans. See Si-fan. T'u-fan. Wu-sz'-tsang.

Thinæ. See Si-ngan-fu.

Timor. See Chi-wan.

Timur. See Tieh-muh-er.

Tinghai. See Chau-shan. Chang-kwoh.

Tocaido. See Tung-hai-tau.

Tocharia. See Ho-si.

Tola river. See Ku-lun.

Tolonnor. See K'au-peh-tau. To-lun-noh-rh.

Tonquin. See Ming-iu. Tung-king.

Toumets. See Sui-yuen-ching. Tu-meh-teh.

Tourbeths. See Tu-rh-peh-teh.

Treaty-ports of China. See Chi-fau. Chin-kiang. Fuh-chau. Han-k'au. Hia-men. Hwang-pu. Ki-lung. Kiu-kiang. Kwang-chau-fu. Ning-po-fu. Niu-chwang. Shan-t'u. Shang-hai. Tai-wan. Tan-sui. Tung-ning. Tang-chau-fu. T'ien-tsin. Yen-t'ai. Ying-t'z'.

Triad Society. See San-hoh-hwui.

Trincomalee. See Ku-ma-lah.

Tsakhar. See Chah-ha-rh.

Ts'i chau. See Tsi-nan-fu.

Tsiampa. See Chen-ching. Chen-pi. P'ing-shun-chin. Shi-pi.

Tsiando. See Chah-muh-to-ching.

Tsitsihar. See Heh-lung-kiang-ching. Tsi-tsi-ha-rh-ching.

Tuchetu. See K'eh-rh-k'eh-t'u-sié-t'u.

T'u-tah. See Yen-tah.

Tuguchuk. See Sui-ting-ching.

Tungâni insurrection. See Ho-tien-ching.

Tungusic tribes. See K'i-tan. Mieh-t'sien. Nu-chih. Sien-pi. Suh-shin-shi. Tah-tah-rh. Tung-hu.

Tung-yu-i. See Yu-i.

Turcomans. See Turkmans.

Turfan. See Ho-chau. Kau-chang. Tu-lu-fan-ting. T'sing-hai.

Turk city. See Tah-rh-ki-ching.

Turkestan (Chinese or Eastern). See Hwui-kiang. Sin-kiang. T'ien-shan-nan-lu. Tuh-ho-lo.

Turkey. See Tu-rh-koh.

Turkic tribes. See Chó-sz'-kwoh. Hiun-yuh. Hiung-nu. Hwui-k'i. Nu-i. Peh-yang. Sah-kia. San-jung. Tuh-kiueh. San-yu, or Tan-yu, and Oh-shi.

Turkmans. See Hung-mau-hwui-tsz'. Tu-po-lo-men.

Tycoon. See Kung-fang. T'ai-kwan. Tsiang-kiun.

Tykes. See Tih.

U

Uchang. See Wu-chang-kwoh.

Uigurs. See Hwui-teh. Hwui-hwui. Hwui-kuh. Kau-chó. Pih-chen.

Ugro-tataric tribes. See Juh. Kau-chó. Kiang. Peh-lan.

Ulgunkash. See Yuh-lung-ho.

Uliasutai. See Wu-li-ya-su-t'ai.

Urats. See Wu-lah-tih.

Urga. See Ku-lun. Mai-mai-chin.
Uriankai tribes. See Tang-nu-wu-liang-hai.
Urumtsi. See Tih-hwa-chau.
Usbeks. See Hwui-heh. Kau-ché.
Ushi. See Wei-t'u-kwoh. Wu-shih-ching. Yung-ning-ching.
Usuri river. See Wu-su-li. Yu-p'i-tah-tsz'.

V

Vernöe. See K'eh-shih-kieh-rh ching.

W

Whampoa. See Hwang-pu.
White desert of China. See Lo-to-keh ching.
Wongpoo. See Hwang-p'u.
Wonin. See Wang-jin.
Wuchang. See Ngoh-chú. T'ung-ting-hu.
Wullanghai tribes. See Tang-nu-wu-liang-hai.

Y

Yachi. See Ta-li-fu.
Yacsa See Yá-keh-sáh.
Yah-tah. See Yen-tah.
Yangchow. See Poh-lo. Yang-chau.
Yangtsz' river. See Chang-kiang. Heh-shwui. Kiang-shwui. Kin-sha-kiang. King-kiang. Lu-kiang. Ma-hu-kiang. Min-kiang. Ta-kiang. Tu-kiang. Wan-kiang. Yang-tsz'-kiang. Shuh-kiang.
Yaritsangbo river. See Ya-lu-tsang-pu.
Yarkand. See Yeh-rh-kiang-ching. Sha-kú-kwoh.
Yeddo. See Kiang-hu.

Yellow river. See A-keh-tan. A-rh-tan. Ho. Hwang-ho. Ho-yuen. Ho-t'au. Sing-suh-hai. Si-ho. Ta-ch'uen.
Yellow sea. See Puh-hai. Tung-yang.
Yemen. See T'ien-fang-kwoh.
Yen. See Yen-king.
Yen-shan. See Yen-king.
Yengihassar. See Yingeshar.
Yengi kurghan. See Yen-kwoh.
Yengu. See Yuen-ku-ching.
Yerkiang. See Sha-ku-kwoh.
Yesso. See Hia-i. Peh-hia-i.
Yingeshar. See I-nai-kwoh. Ying-kih-sha-rh-ching.
Yokohama. See Hung-pin.
Yuen-yuen. See Ju-ju.
Yú's provinces. See K'i-chau. King-chau. Liang-chau. Su-jung. T'sing-chau. Yang-chau. Yen-chau. Yu-chau. Yung-chau.
Yurung kash. See Yuh-lung-ho.
Yu-t'o-li. See San-fuh-tsi.
Yuts. See Ta-yuoh-chí.

Z

Zaitun. See Taitun.
Zardandan. See Kin-ch'i.
Zariavshan. See Sah-ma-rh-han.
Zendavesta. See Po-sz'-king-kiau.
Zhikátsi. See Jeh-hoh-tseh.
Ziákú. See Shuh-chau.
Zoroaster. See Po-sz'-king-kiau.
Zypangu. See Sypangu.